Live a healthier life at a fraction of the cost

EAT WELL ON A DOLLAR A DAY

Bill and Ruth Kaysing

Chronicle Books,  San Francisco

Library of Congress Catalog Card Number: 75-10820
ISBN: 0-87701-066-8

Chronicle Books
870 Market Street
San Francisco
California 94102

Designed by Jon Goodchild
Printed in the United States of America

Other Writings by Bill Kaysing

THE COMPLETE ILLUSTRATED FIRST TIME
  FARMER'S GUIDE
HOW TO LIVE IN THE NEW AMERICA
GREAT HOT SPRINGS OF THE WEST
THE ROBIN HOOD HANDBOOK
INTELLIGENT MOTORCYCLING
HOW YOU CAN STOP SMOKING AND ENJOY IT

To Wendy, Jill
and
Ruth Kaysing
with gratitude.

They helped me
so I could
help others.

Contents

Wild hickory nuts

Author's note

Until I was forty (I am now fifty-two), I lived on a diet of plastic foods. It was a rare day in South Pasadena when, as a growing boy, I didn't consume at least four or five of my favorite candy bars. Fueled by these hunger-stoppers plus plenty of canned corn, hot tamales, and ice cream, I dragged through adolescence like a tired snail. I usually felt dull, sluggish, and hungry.

Not long after the Japanese invaded Pearl Harbor, I began to eat the United States Navy's fare. Big deal. Still no feelings of good health and exuberance. And I went from bad to worse. In 1950 I worked as an insurance adjuster in lovely Los Angeles, and I started my day three hundred and sixty-five times a year with a cream puff. Looking back, I'm sure that the physical and mental collapse I finally experienced was due to my abominable diet. But I *still* didn't wise up until about ten years ago when my family began talking to me about wheat germ and yogurt and co-author Ruth showed me the way to good health and high spirits with a natural foods diet. Since that turn-around in my eating habits, I've never had a cold or a sick day. My enthusiasm and excitement at just being alive and feeling great are unlimited. And that feeling is reflected in my work; I have never been as productive as I am now.

So take heart when you read these pages. If it can happen to me, it can certainly happen to you.

Bill Kaysing

Introduction

uthors often give their works-in-progress nicknames. This one had two: "Eat" and "The Radical Gourmet." I like the latter because it implies that people are going to have to take what amounts to a radical political stance in order to fight against the blandishments of Madison Avenue and the lure of the supermarkets. We are increasingly required to fight the good fight in order to maintain our basic right to eat well for a reasonable amount of money. This means that we must constantly search for alternatives to the down-the-drain methods of buying and preparing food that the media and the food industries encourage.

If you are browsing in a book store and are just riffling through this book out of curiosity, consider this anecdote before you put the book down.

Susan Savvy goes on a marketing expedition and buys the following items for $5.00:

•	Honey	1 pound	$ .65
•	Potatoes	10 pounds	.70
•	Cheese	1 pound	1.10
•	Whole grain wheat	10 pounds	1.30
•	Peanut butter	1 pound	.75
•	Dry beans	1 pound	.50
			$5.00

Here's what Pat Programmed buys at the local Plastic Food Mart for the same price:

•	Sugar	5 pounds	$2.35
•	White flour	5 pounds	1.25
•	Hamburger additive	2 portions	1.40
			$5.00

Susan obtained twenty-four pounds of healthful, basic, bulk foods for her five dollars. Naturally prices vary throughout the country and according to the season. These were obtained as the book went to press in Santa Cruz, California. They are the listed prices at a local natural food store.

To assist the reader in comparing the actual food values in the purchases made by Sue and Pat, here are reproductions from a remarkably valuable pamphlet titled *Nutritive Value of Foods*. It is Home and Garden Bulletin Number 72 issued by the United States Department of Agriculture. To obtain a copy write to the U.S.D.A., Washington, D.C. 20250, for availability and price of a copy for your own use.

The reader can draw his own conclusions as to which shopper got the most food value for their five bucks.

Need I say more? If so, be apprised of what we're up against.

Nutrients

Nutrients:	What they do:	Where they are found:
Protein	Builds and repairs all tissues Helps form antibodies to fight infection	Meat, fish, poultry, egg Milk, cheese Dried beans and peas Nuts, peanut butter Cereals, breads
Fat	Supplies a large amount of energy in small amount of food Supplies essential fatty acids	Fat in meat Butter Salad oils, dressings Cooking oil, salt pork, bacon drippings
Carbohydrate	Supplies energy Helps the body use other nutrients	Cereals, breads Corn, grits, oats, rice Spaghetti, macaroni, noodles Molasses, honey, syrup, jams

Nutrients:	What they do:	Where they are found:
Minerals		
Calcium	Helps build bones and teeth Helps blood clot Helps muscles and nerves react normally	Milk, yogurt Cheese Mustard and turnip greens Collards, kale Canned salmon and mackerel
Phosphorus	Helps build bones and teeth Helps control the rate at which energy is released	Milk Meat, fish, poultry, eggs Cereals
Iron	Combines with protein to make hemoglobin, the red substance in the blood that carries oxygen to the cells	Liver, other meats and eggs Dried beans and peas Whole grain cereals and breads Dark green leafy vegetables Molasses

Water

Also essential, even though many people do not think of it as food. Water helps in carrying the nutrients to cells and waste products away, in building tissues, regulating body temperature, aiding digestion and replacing daily water loss.

Nutrients:	What they do:	Where they are found:
Vitamins		
Essential for body growth, for resisting infection and for keeping the body functioning properly. All vitamins needed for good health can be found in food.		
Vitamin A	Helps keep skin clear and smooth Helps eyes adjust to dim light Helps keep lining of mouth, nose, throat and digestive tract healthy and resistant to infection	Liver, egg yolk Dark green leafy and yellow vegetables Deep yellow fruits Whole milk Yogurt Butter
Thiamin or Vitamin B1	Promotes good appetite and digestion Helps keep nerves in healthy condition Helps change substances in food into energy for work	Whole grain cereals and breads Milk, cheese Lean meat and variety meat like liver, heart, kidney
Riboflavin or Vitamin B2	Helps cells use oxygen Helps keep vision clear Helps keep skin around mouth and nose smooth	Whole grain cereals and breads Milk, cheese Lean meat and variety meat like liver heart, kidney

Nutrients:	What they do:	Where they are found:
Niacin	Helps keep nervous system healthy Helps body cells use oxygen to produce energy Helps to maintain the health of the skin, tongue and digestive system	Whole grain cereals and breads Peanuts, peanut butter Lean meat, poultry, fish Peas, beans
Ascorbic Acid or Vitamin C	Helps maintain intercell structure Strengthens walls of blood vessels Helps in healing wounds Helps resist infection	Oranges, grapefruits, limes, lemons Strawberries, cantaloupes Collards, mustard greens, cabbage, green peppers Potatoes
Vitamin D	Helps the body absorb calcium Helps build strong bones	Vitamin D fortified milk Cod or halibut liver oil Salt water fish, mackerel, canned salmon

The American food industry is a $110 billion a year business. Somewhere between the farmer, who gets $30 billion, and the consumer, who pays the $110 billion, there is a large leak of $80 billion. In other words, the middlemen who promote and sell the food and control the prices we pay for it make a *gross* profit of $80 billion a year. It is the purpose of this book to encourage you to help reduce this leak or plug it up altogether by providing two kinds of information: how to eat what your body needs and wants (not what the industry says it should need and want); and how to avoid paying into the pockets of the middleman.

To eat well you must learn how to outwit some very clever minds. The food-industry moguls and their hired guns, the dirty rats on Madison Avenue, are very good at what they do. They managed to convince a huge proportion of the American people that we are getting our money's worth when we buy processed foods. They have accomplished this monumental feat (monumental considering the evidence to the contrary) in most cases by suppressing or simply ignoring the truth. To help you deal with these rascals, culprits, and con men, the bulk of this book will elaborate on these basic rules:

1. Plan on changing your entire way of life regarding food. No half-way measures will do if you really want to eat for less than a dollar a day.

2. Develop a sense of humor as well as a sense of strategy. Think of yourself as a guerrilla in a funny/serious war with rats who are trying to profit from your presumed gullibility. But keep in mind that the last laugh will be yours, since you are fully capable of using your head in finding out the truth on your own.

3. Stay out of supermarkets except when shopping for fresh foods and possibly dairy products.

4. Search out and buy from alternative food sources (I cite some good ones in this book).

5. Plan on keeping lots of bulk foods in your home at all times. That way you will reduce your shopping trips and will be protected in case of disaster.

6. Be open-minded. Try new foods, both wild and domestic.

7. Plant a garden; the bigger it is the better for your pocketbook. There are good books on the subject in your local library and book store, and more are coming out all the time.

8. Learn about harvest times for local crops. Take a weekend drive in the country and make it a food-gathering trip.

9. Think of meat as a condiment, not as a staple.

10. Give up sugar and all sugar-containing products. It's easier to do than you may think, and the reasons for doing it are pressing, as you will learn.

11. Buy international cookbooks. Find out what people in other cultures eat and try their recipes.

12. Eat raw foods or let things cook themselves. Save time and energy (yours and the kind you pay for).

13. Eat less. Determine your own minimum requirements and keep to them.

14. Don't waste anything.

15. Make your own convenience foods. You can even make money doing this if you're creative and enterprising enough.

As a side note, I want to emphasize that this book takes a positive approach to shopping and food preparation. It was designed to encourage you to change your ways by providing creative suggestions. Rather than labor the specific evils of packaged and processed foods, I refer you to Adelle Davis' *Let's Eat Right to Keep Fit* (New American Library), and D. Sanford's *Hot War on the Consumer* (Pitman).

Now read on for specific information. You'll feel better just knowing that you can win at the game the food industry plays with you for their profit.

PART 1
HOW TO SHOP
ON A DOLLAR
A DAY

What to buy to stock your pantry

What You'll Learn:
What to buy for maximum
economy and nutrition. Typical staples
and basic foods.

Pioneering Americans learned how to ensure an adequate food supply for their families against all sorts of disasters and unpredictable events. They maintained a pantry with stocks of basic items such as grains, beans, nuts, and seeds. Then, no matter what happened—floods, Indian wars, poor harvests—they could survive *and* keep their strength up.

Anyone can set up a pantry at any time and almost anywhere. Create a space, build some shelves if you have to, find or buy some sealable containers, and with the basic staples listed below plus a supply of fresh foods to combine them with you're all set. The Chinese and Mexican styles of cooking revolve around a well-stocked pantry with great success both economically and nutritionally. Take a look at some Chinese and Mexican cookbooks to get a sense of how you can work from the basics in your pantry to produce a great variety of inexpensive, healthful, and delicious meals. Your cooking will be simple and direct—almost nothing to it if you've stocked up thoroughly. And you will have automatically produced a healthy food environment for yourself and your family.

The rules to follow when setting up your pantry are simple:
- Buy basic foods that are easy to store without refrigeration.
- Buy in bulk.
- Avoid all packaged foods.
- Buy fresh vegetables and fruits to combine with your pantry staples.

The amount of purchase will vary from family to family, but we recommend buying as much as your storage space and budget permit. For example, a family of four could profit by purchasing five hundred pounds of wheat at one time, thereby undoubtedly getting a discount. It can be stored in clean cans, bottles or metal lined bins to prevent mice and rat attacks. With that purchase alone (remember, it increases fourfold when cooked) the family would have a reserve of more than a ton of excellent food on hand. If not eaten, it can be bartered for other foods, planted in the spring, parched (lightly roasted) as a snack or otherwise put to good use.

Here's a good general rule: Keep enough food stored to provide ten times the body weight of each family member (a 150-pound man needs 1500 pounds of food per year). This would ensure a one-year reserve of basic foods. But again, remember that dry foods make up to three to five times their dry weight. Thus, less is needed as long as a plentiful supply of pure water is available.

Now to the specifics of what to buy to stock your pantry. You'll find recipes and suggestions on how to use these foods in subsequent chapters.

Whole Grain Wheat

Basic to most diets, wheat can be freshly ground for bread, rolls, pancakes, and other baked goods. It can be boiled whole (or slightly cracked) for cereal. Or it can simply be soaked to grow sprouts. However you choose to use it, a substantial quantity of whole grain wheat will provide a strong and solid foundation for your home food supply. Suggestions on how to use wheat will be found throughout this book. A hundred-pound sack is recommended.

Cost as we go to press is $13.00 at bulk food stores.

Brown Rice

More rice is consumed in the world than any other grain. There's a good reason for this: rice is high in nutritional value. Although it's somewhat difficult to grow, billions of hard-working people throughout the world consider rice to be an imperative staple. And so

A Kernel of Wheat

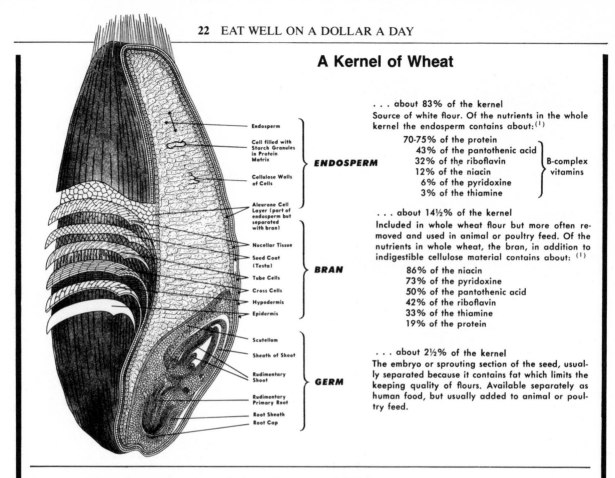

. . . about 83% of the kernel
Source of white flour. Of the nutrients in the whole kernel the endosperm contains about:[1]

ENDOSPERM
- 70-75% of the protein
- 43% of the pantothenic acid
- 32% of the riboflavin
- 12% of the niacin
- 6% of the pyridoxine
- 3% of the thiamine

B-complex vitamins

. . . about 14½% of the kernel
Included in whole wheat flour but more often removed and used in animal or poultry feed. Of the nutrients in whole wheat, the bran, in addition to indigestible cellulose material contains about: [1]

BRAN
- 86% of the niacin
- 73% of the pyridoxine
- 50% of the pantothenic acid
- 42% of the riboflavin
- 33% of the thiamine
- 19% of the protein

. . . about 2½% of the kernel
The embryo or sprouting section of the seed, usually separated because it contains fat which limits the keeping quality of flours. Available separately as human food, but usually added to animal or poultry feed.

GERM

Diagram labels: Endosperm; Cell filled with Starch Granules in Protein Matrix; Cellulose Walls of Cells; Aleurone Cell Layer (part of endosperm but separated with bran); Nucellar Tissue; Seed Coat (Testa); Tube Cells; Cross Cells; Hypodermis; Epidermis; Scutellum; Sheath of Shoot; Rudimentary Shoot; Rudimentary Primary Root; Root Sheath; Root Cap

Brown Rice Compared to Other Types of Rice

Composition of Rice (per 100 g or 3 oz))

	Brown Rice		White Rice		Enriched White Rice		Converted Rice (Enriched)	
1. Protein	7.5 g		6.7 g	90%	6.7 g	90%	7.4 g	99%
2. Minerals								
Calcium	32 mg		24 mg	75%	24 mg	75%	60 mg	190%
Phosphorous	221 mg		94 mg	43%	94 mg	43%	200 mg	90%
Iron	1.6 mg		0.8 mg	50%	2.9 mg	180%	2.9 mg	180%
Potassium	214 mg		92 mg	43%	92 mg	43%	50 mg	70%
Sodium	9 mg		5 mg	56%	5 mg	56%	9 mg	100%
3. Vitamins								
Thiamin	0.34 mg		0.07 mg	21%	0.44 mg	130%	0.44 mg	130%
Riboflavin	0.05 mg		0.03 mg	60%	0.03 mg	60%	0.03 mg	60%
Niacin	4.7 mg		1.6 mg	34%	3.5 mg	74%	3.5 mg	74%

will you once you enjoy it cooked in many different ways and benefit from its valuable minerals and vitamins.

Never buy white rice. The best part of its grain, the outer hull, has been polished away and used (hard to believe) to soak up oil on service station floors!

More on the uses of rice will follow, but be sure to try it steamed or boiled for breakfast with dates or raisins.

Cost: $40.00
per 100-pound sack.

Oats

Oats are often thought of merely as oatmeal, but they have quite a lot going for them. First of all, they are usually quite inexpensive, especially when you buy a nice fat 100-pound sack of rolled oats at your feed store. (Won't it look reassuring in your pantry?) Nutritionally, brown rice and several other grains are more potent than oats, but just think of all the goodies you can make with a plentiful supply of oats: oatmeal cookies, with plenty of walnuts and perhaps some raisins, oatmeal pancakes, and tasty, economical meat loaves. Or how about some beautifully browned oatmeal bread or muffins, oatmeal cake and hot cherry pudding made with cherries you picked yourself in some farmer's orchard? So don't consider your pioneer pantry complete without an easy-to-store sack of oats.

Cost: $9.50 per 100-pound sack.

Barley

Barley is one of the most neglected basic grains. There's no real reason for this; barley is a nutty-tasting, solid-bodied grain that can add a lot to your daily menu at extremely low cost. Canned-soup makers load their meat-based soups with it because they know it's cheap and richly flavored. But don't buy it manufactured into a high-priced item; just go down and pick up a sack or two for yourself. Incidentally barley is a basic ingredient in beer.

Cost: $9.50 per 100-pound sack.

Millet

"Me, eat bird seed?" That *could* be the plaintive cry of someone just introduced to this grain; most of us do associate it with bird-seed mix, and the little round grains do resemble something that a parakeet would love. What most people in America don't know is that millet, an easily grown staple, is an important and basic food to hundreds of millions of people worldwide. It's not the tastiest grain going, but it can be added to other foods to increase nutritional value. Your soups and stews will have more body and textural interest if you simply add a handful or so of millet before simmering. Millet is often cooked with stock and used as a side dish with fish or chicken. It even makes a fine candy; just cook it for a time with honey, pour it out to cool, and cut it into bars.

Cost: $22.00 per 100-pound sack.

Rye

Rye is best-known here as a main ingredient in bread, but it is a well-accepted grain in Europe, particularly in Russia. Many experts claim that dark bread made mainly from rye flour is far healthier than any other kind. Rye bread certainly has a distinctive and unique flavor and goes well with many robust, peasant-style dishes. Red cabbage and sausages demand a rye accompaniment. Rye may be purchased in whole-grain form or as ready-ground flour; either way it's a solid staple that should be in a well-stocked pantry.

Cost: $55.00 per 100-pound sack.

Corn

So highly regarded by the Aztecs that they often cast its image in solid gold, corn has always been and still is a world favorite. Buy it in whole-kernel form as shown here. In this way, it's undegerminated so you get full food value. You can make your own fresh cornmeal in your own blender. Stock up on corn; it's inexpensive and tasty.

Cost: $9.50 per 100-pound sack.

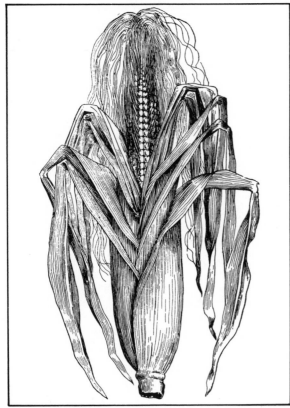

Soybeans

Truly a wonder legume, the soybean is a must for any larder that combines high-quality nutrition with low cost. Soybeans are so important to any diet that a separate chapter is devoted to them later in this book. Soybeans will make a dollar-a-day diet possible with money to spare.

The Chinese have had many thousands of years to develop a national diet, and even a philosophy of life, around soybeans. The amazing variety of dishes they make from soy beans will astound you unless you are already familiar with them. But rather than overstate our case in this brief introduction, turn to Chapter 14 and see what a bonanza of good nutrition and good taste you'll find in soybeans and their related products.

Cost: $17.00 per 100-pound sack.

Beans in general

Pinto, lima, red, kidney, great northern, and navy are but a few of the many varieties of delicious and nutritious beans. Beans vary in nutritional content, but they often make a fine substitute for the proteins found in meat. Further, they can be prepared in an infinite variety of ways. Beans are usually inexpensive, but their prices vary with availability. Become aware of price fluctuations. Simply wait out high prices and buy when the beans you want become reasonable again. Because they store well, buy a lot when the price is down; you'll feel a great sense of security with so much good food tucked away.

Cost: Average $40.00 to $50.00 per 100-pound sack.

Split peas

Split peas are closely related to the bean family. They should definitely be considered an important part of your pioneer pantry. They're easily storable, nutritious, relatively inexpensive, and are always ready to go into the soup or stew pot to make a good dish better. They're great alone too, simmered with a ham bone and lots of onions in the classic split-pea soup.

Cost: $32.00 per 100-pound sack.

Potatoes

Potatoes rank next in line with the long-term storables such as grains and beans. They are much more valuable nutritionally than commonly believed and they're not even fattening if you go easy on the butter and sauces. These delicious tubers can be a mainstay to your diet; all they need is a chance to prove their merit

Nutrient Yield Charts

For One Dollar Spent

As you review these charts, note how *low* meat ranks in nutrient yield per dollar. Conversely, a simple, low cost food like potatoes speaks very well for itself.

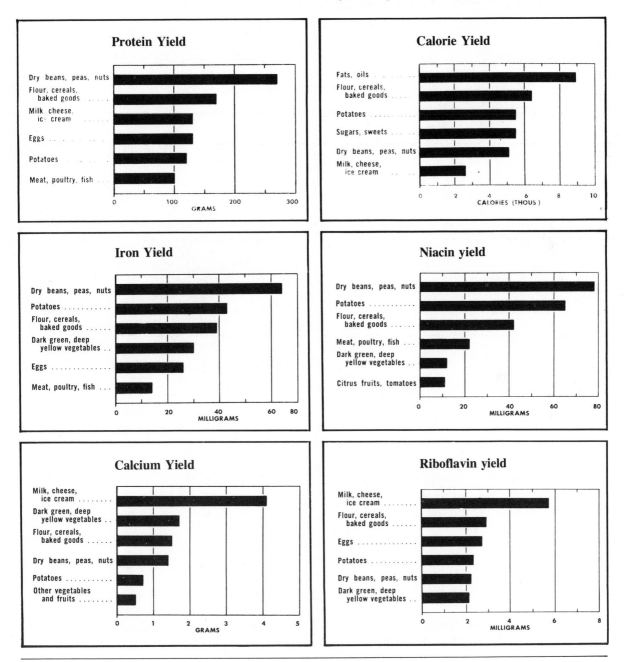

through creative cooking. Spuds are important enough to warrant a chapter of their own. See Chapter 13 for suggestions on how to use them.

Cost: $6.00 per 100 pounds.

Onions

Onions are a friendly companion to potatoes and lots of other good things. They should rank high on your priority list for staple items. Recent studies indicate that they are valuable in maintaining good health and preventing many types of nutritionally related disabilities, so eat lots of these fine, easily stored vegetables. There are virtually unlimited ways of preparing onions, from just plain sliced and raw to elegant French style onion soup with cheese and croutons.

There are dozens of varieties of onions: red, white, yellow, Bermuda, and green, to mention a few of the most popular. Major variance is in strength of flavor; the bigger onions, such as the large red ones, have a less pungent taste. Some of these are so mild that they can be eaten raw like apples. Yellow onions of medium size are probably the most commonly used in cooking. Green onions are flavorful and healthy; they can be added raw to salads or used as a garnish.

Cost: Average $10.00 per 100-pounds.

Garlic

This tasty bulb is a smaller, stronger relative of the onion. Long a standby of French and Italian cooks, you'll find it a most useful adjunct to basic food cookery. For example, added to rice pilaf (recipe later) garlic makes an otherwise bland food delicious.

Here are the most common ways of utilizing this flavorful and healthful food: For salads, peel and halve a clove of garlic and rub sides of wooden salad bowl, or simply soak a clove in your homemade oil and vinegar salad dressing. For spaghetti and macaroni sauces and similar dishes, peel, slice and saute in butter. Then add other ingredients.

Shallots, a less strong relative of garlic, can be used in similar ways.

Cost: Varies, about $1.00 per lb.

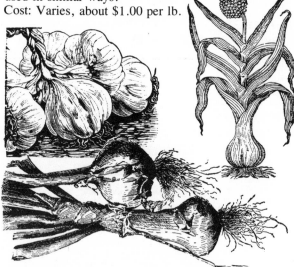

Cheese. An excellent source of protein.

Nuts. A source of protein plus fats, minerals, and vitamins.

Raw certified milk. Another high-protein food.

Vegetables. Organic and fresh vegetables provide almost everything needed for good health.

Fruits. Vitamin and mineral content alone make them a must for a healthy diet.

Eggs. Use only natural eggs from farm-raised (not assembly-line) chickens.

Seeds. They contain the best balance of nutrients in nature.

Sprouts. Even more nutritional value than seeds!

Honey. A natural sugar, but go easy.

Blackstrap molasses. Energy plus minerals; a natural sweet.

Wheat germ. The richest known source of Vitamin E.

Alfalfa. Very rich in minerals.

Bone meal. A good source of calcium and phosphorus.

Desiccated liver. Lots of B_{12} plus other vitamins and minerals.

Brewer's yeast. Contains concentrated proteins.

Fish liver oils. Contain substantial amounts of Vitamins A and D.

Rose hips. Contains ten times the Vitamin C in other foods.

Kelp. An excellent source of trace minerals.

Meat. A good protein source if it's high-quality and pure.

Poultry. A protein source; again, avoid chemical birds.

Fish. Protein equal to that in meat and eggs; lots of phosphorus.

Natural vegetable oils. The real stuff contains valuable blood components.

Herb teas. Fine home remedies for what ails you.

Yogurt. Easily digested; high in vitamins.

Vitamin Supplements. Use as needed, but only from natural sources.

Soybeans. Rank with meat, milk, fish and eggs as a protein source.

Raw juices. Great substitutes for coffee and tea.

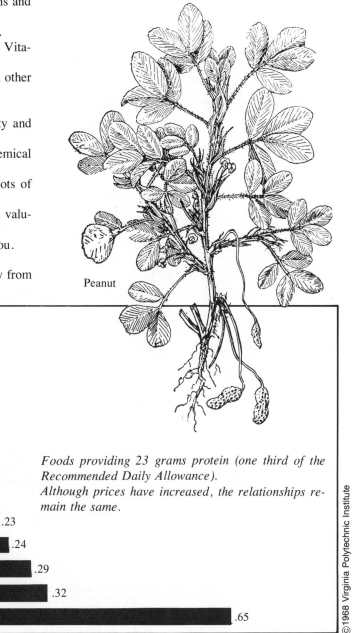

Peanut

Food Cost Comparison

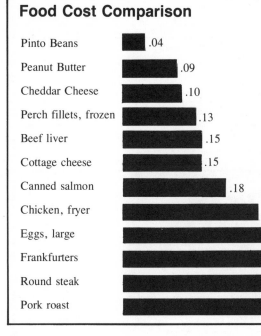

Pinto Beans	.04
Peanut Butter	.09
Cheddar Cheese	.10
Perch fillets, frozen	.13
Beef liver	.15
Cottage cheese	.15
Canned salmon	.18
Chicken, fryer	.23
Eggs, large	.24
Frankfurters	.29
Round steak	.32
Pork roast	.65

Foods providing 23 grams protein (one third of the Recommended Daily Allowance).
Although prices have increased, the relationships remain the same.

Robert Altman

Where to shop and how to do it

What you'll learn:
Alternatives to supermarkets—wholesale grocers, natural food stores, feed stores, and produce markets—and how to use them.

Recently, on a family outing my wife went into a supermarket to buy some food for lunch. When she returned empty-handed a few minutes later, I asked her why. Everything in that store was wrapped in plastic. Two slices of phony meat loaded with preservatives for 89 cents! I just couldn't bear to waste our money on it." This incident left a profound impression on us. It made us realize that it's becoming less and less possible to buy something—anything—in a conventional grocery store that's worth buying, let alone worth *eating*. Consumers are bearing the brunt of this trend more heavily every day. Artificial, heavily processed non-food sealed in plastic or metal is junk for robots, not people. But there are ways to avoid the food-for-profit conspiracy.

First of all, make sure you know the meaning of the following terms:

Cooperative Buying: Two or more people pool their money and buy as a group. They share in accordance with their contributions of money and time.

Wholesale Buying: Buying at grocers' prices. Sometimes the discounts are substantial; at other times they are minimal but still worth the effort.

Bulk Buying: Buying in large quantities. Not necessarily wholesale buying, since many retail sales are made in bulk quantities; for example, you can buy a 100-pound sack of whole grain wheat at many feed stores or grain mills, and outlets are opening up advertising "survival foods" in bulk quantities.

In Berkeley, California, two families I know occupy two separate floors of a huge, old-fashioned house. One is the family of an engineer and one of an attorney. These people are well-educated and have learned to apply their intelligence and training to the problem of high food costs. First, they pooled their grocery money. Second, they went to a local wholesale grocer; that is, the grocer who provides staple foods to small "Mom and Pop" grocery stores. The small-store grocers come in regularly to buy a sack of this, a half a case of that, a wheel or two of cheese, etc. The terms are usually cash on the proverbial barrelhead. The attorney and engineer told the wholesale grocer that they, too, would like to buy wholesale. Since they agreed to abide by the cash terms, the wholesaler was pleased to cooperate. The families now buy canned vegetables by the case for a substantial percentage less than individual shelf prices. They buy 100-pound sacks of dried beans, brown rice, potatoes, onions, and other basic staples such as wheels of cheese and spices in bulk. The big house has a large storage room or pantry and this has begun to look like a wholesale grocery facility itself! Just think of the savings these families are making! They buy cooperatively and in quantity and share the purchases equally. For example, by purchasing powdered milk in 100-pound sacks, they have driven the cost down to less than 50 percent of the boxed price. By purchasing cheese in wheels and cutting and wrapping it into individual portions themselves, they pay about 70 percent less than the retail price for this important protein source. During periods when foods are abundant due to seasonal harvests, they buy boxes of apples and pears, lugs of tomatoes and peppers, and sacks of staples such as sweet potatoes and popcorn. On every possible occasion the families join forces and go into the nearby rural areas to pick fruit and nuts direct from the farmers' trees.

It's apparent that by buying cooperatively in bulk quantities and at wholesale prices this team has discovered a way to save thousands of dollars a year! In the process, they have learned two things: (1) It's fun for the whole family (children love to play grocer, cutting and wrapping cheese and drying fruits on the roof); and (2) Everyone becomes more skillful with experi-

THE GREAT FOOD-BUYING CONSPIRACY

PEOPLE'S OFFICE
BERKELEY, CALIFORNIA

The food-buying co-ops take cooperation among members to make them work but savings are really something (20–50%). They function this way:

1. Neighborhood groups of five to eight living units get together and send representatives to a Thursday night central meeting. Every adult pays a non-refundable, one-time kitty fee of $2.00 or more as a cushion for fronting the money to buy things. At the meeting, orders are taken from the representatives of each group for fruit and vegetables.

At 6:00 AM Saturday morning, three or four people go down to the Farmer's Market in San Francisco and buy organically grown fruits and vegetables in boxes or crates and save lots of money.

Between 10:30 and 12:30 everyone comes and gets his stuff at a central location. The price per lb. is a bit marked up to cover waste—there's always left-over stuff since you have to over-buy a little (crates come in standard amounts). Mark-ups might be 1¢/lb. for items under 10¢/lb., 2¢ under 20¢/lb. 3¢ under 30¢/lb. etc.

You'll need:

1. large vehicles (two if over 30 living units are buying).
2. Two bookkeeper-cashiers and a table.
3. Space-two or three spaces in your parking lot.
4. Two or three scales ($1–$3 used at Value Village in Richmond or Oakland or at Flea Markets, baby scales are best).
5. CASH to pay the farmers—no checks accepted.
6. Paper bags and boxes so people can carry their stuff home.
7. One person to dispose of left-overs (see "Dry Goods" below).

2. Domestic and imported cheese at a 20% discount (on 20 lbs. or more) is available from the CheeseBoard on Vine near Walnut in Berkeley.

The order, composed of each group's orders combined is phoned in on TUESDAY MORNING (make sure and tell them you're a new group), and picked up at 8:00 PM Friday night. It is paid for then.

The cheese is cut up and weighed on Friday night, and put into packages for each group. It is distributed TO GROUP REPRESENTATIVES on Saturday morning with produce or dry goods (see below). Group reps pay the cashier for their group's order.

You'll need two-three people to handle cheese.

3. Once a month or so you may want to buy good, organic dry goods. The prices are well below even non-organically grown things bought in the supermarket. You may want to contact Bill O'Connell or Marcia Binder at FOR THE LOVE OF PEOPLE, on Telegraph in Oakland just this side of the new freeway overpass on the right as you head south. (No phone). They are a health food co-op and they get good things at low prices if you buy in large quantities (like 100 lbs. of flour, 30 lbs. of raisins, etc.

FOR THE LOVE OF PEOPLE needs our help in going and getting the stuff, as their truck can't hold too much. Contact other co-ops to find out when everybody's going, and a caravan of People's Co-ops can go together to the wholesalers.

Sometimes dry goods can be purchased in large quantities at very reasonable prices therefore:

1. Storage space is needed, preferably a kitchen or room with a sink. Maybe you could wheedle out a basement room from your landlord or manager (ask the latter to join, if he's a resident!) near where you distribute produce.

   You also need plastic-bag lined garbage cans and five gallon ice cream containers for storage, as well as ladies, scoops (cut out plastic bleach bottles are great!) and funnels. Also jars for honey, peanut butter and oil.

2. Lots of front money is needed—one way is to sell $5.00 or more worth of SCRIPT to members, enough to cover the cost completely each time you make a dry goods run. Members then pay in script for dry goods!

The same price mark-up system as for produce is advised. There is always waste.

Dry goods are distributed at the same time as produce.

Bookkeeping for dry goods is easy with script. Script in $1.00 amounts can be used, with purchases which come to under or over the even dollar being paid in script and change You'll need one or two cashiers, and one or two people to help weigh things out. (P.S. Script could be paper, coins, special stamped objects, you name it.)

GENERAL HINTS: In the case of produce and dry goods, everyone weighs his own and tallies his bill, with the cashier checking the addition. Equal participation and equal responsibility. It works if you're careful to be accurate. Cheese is another story. Cutting is tricky as cheese varies in density from one kind to another. Waste is more costly at 70-90¢/ lb. Produce buyers should try to get to know the farmers and should draw up the price list on the way back. A blackboard is handy for listing prices.

ence. Bargaining becomes sharper when you've had a few sessions behind you.

In summary, we suggest that you consider all *three* aspects of this method, cooperative, wholesale, and bulk buying. However, if for any reason you can't manage all three, then at least try one or two. A single person, for example, can buy in reasonably large bulk quantities. And single people can join the cooperative food groups springing up in great numbers all over America. Check with your local natural food store or community action groups for co-ops in your area. If you don't find one, think about starting one of your own.

Some years back a wholesale meat market in Los Angeles let it be known that it was willing to sell meat at wholesale prices to members of the local musicians' union and their families. If you belong to a union, perhaps you could approach one of your local meat wholesalers with an offer to have all of your members buy from him. It's hardly likely he'd turn down the chance to sell meat to individuals if their total number were sufficient to represent large quantity buying.

Wholesale grocers often require a resale permit number, which is what you obtain when you take out a license to operate a business in some states. If you run up against this requirement, try to find someone who has a relative or friend with such a resale permit number that he would be willing to let your group use from time to time. If all else fails, you could even start up a small grocery store of your own. Many people have done this. Business licenses aren't too expensive, and a tiny hole-in-the-wall grocery can actually return enough profit to pay more than its expenses. Thus you would have an unlimited source of food at wholesale prices. Here's an area in which your resourcefulness and ingenuity will pay off in big returns.

Natural Food Stores

These quaint places are springing up everywhere. They are usually manned by aware people who are more interested in selling nutritious food than making a profit. If you've never been in one, you have a pleasant surprise in store. First, they're usually relaxed and imaginatively decorated, and there's a feeling of, "O.K., let's have some fun while we're shopping and talking about healthful food."

Robert Altman

The shopkeepers, men or women, are usually healthy and energetic; after all, they eat what they sell. Ask them what to buy. They'll know which items are particularly plentiful at the time, which ones will make up a special-company meal, and which foods to buy for more energy.

Speaking of energy foods, you'll find big bins of natural grains—wheat, rice, oats, barley, millet, and corn. This is the place to stock your pantry. The store may have a grinder, hand or electric, so you can fresh-grind your purchase.

And for the best tasting and most nutritious peanut butter you'll ever eat, try grinding your own from fresh raw peanuts in most any natural food store. Surprisingly, it's cheaper than supermarket commercial brands.

Look up your nearest natural food outlet under "Natural," "Health," "Organic," or similar listings in the phone book yellow pages. Avoid stores that only carry elaborately packaged items such as bottles of vitamins and over-priced, over-processed cereals. Health food stores have been known to play the food-for-profit game as well as supermarkets. Write to *Prevention* Magazine, Emmaus, Pennsylvania 18049, for a list of good stores.

Feed Stores

I grew up thinking that a feed store was for animals exclusively. Then one day I noticed that the whole wheat I had purchased for my horses looked both appealing and nutritious. If good old Pixie, my quarter horse mare, thrived on it, why couldn't we? I took a small amount home and put it through my old-fashioned meat grinder, fine blade. Suddenly it resembled something that I knew well, a packaged hot cereal made from wheat. Hey, I thought, have I been. . .? Yes, I was paying a lot more for the grocery-store version of wheat cereal than I should have been—eight times more, as a matter of fact. In a fancy little box it cost about 80 cents a pound; in its natural, untouched and more healthful state, it cost about a dime at the time of this writing.

From that day on, I shared all kinds of grains with gentle Pixie. I found that the feed store I went to could obtain every grain imaginable—oats, rice, corn, millet, barley, plus all kinds of seeds (sunflower, alfalfa,

sesame), and beans, peanuts, and wheat germ. In short, the feed store could provide anything in the basic bulk, unpackaged line. And prices? Lower than I'd ever thought possible. At that time, in 1969, sacks of rolled oats that would last my family for months cost three or four dollars. Now they average about $15, which is still a bargain, considering skyrocketing supermarket

prices. Wheat germ, fresh from the mill was about 15 cents a pound in paper sacks. (Compare that to what you pay for a glass jar of wheat germ in your local supermarket.)

I began saving so much money I thought there must be a Catch 22 in it somewhere. So I asked the feed-store manager about purity. He said, "Bill, if we sold anything that would harm the race horses that eat our products, we'd be out of business in a month." Realizing that I was insured for a lot less than the race horse in the pasture adjoining Pixie's, I stopped worrying.

Of course, there's always a possibility that what you buy there may not be suitable for human consumption without some processing; oats need to be rolled and hulled, for example. But for the most part, everything in a feed and grain store is ready to use. To get you started, here's a recipe that will provide you with a low-cost, natural and healthful breakfast tomorrow morning if you pick up a sack of whole grain wheat at your local feed store today.

Grind the wheat in your old meat grinder or use the blender at high speed. Boil a pint of water; add salt if you wish. Slowly add the fresh-ground wheat, about 4 to 6 ounces depending on whether you want your cereal thin or thick. Stir. Turn down the heat and let it bubble for 10 to 15 minutes with an occasional stir. If desired, add some chopped dates, nuts, or snipped-up dried fruit just before removing from stove.

Voila! You have two large bowls of fresh ground-cereal complete with the original wheat germ. Add some milk or cream, a spoonful of honey, and sit down to a great natural breakfast. Cost? Aside from the things you added, about 4 cents for two half-pound bowls! Compare that 2-cent breakfast of steaming whole wheat with a bowl of pallid, over-priced and over-sugared packaged cereal and draw your own conclusions.

You'll find natural grains in bulk form in stores listed under "Feed," "Hay," "Grain," "Ranch" or "Farm" in the yellow pages.

Produce Markets

When I was a small boy, the Great Depression was in full swing. No Help Wanted signs festooned the stores and shops of the small town, South Pasadena, California, where I lived. My family wasn't poverty-stricken, but low-cost or no-cost food was always welcome. I quickly learned that there was lots of fine food behind grocery stores. For example, the green grocer would peel off a few leaves from each head of lettuce every day to give them a fresh appearance. Once the heads had been reduced to small cannonball size, they were tossed in the out basket. Think of it! Hearts of lettuce for free! After frequenting the backs of stores for a while, I became more sophisticated. I would arrive on the scene just as the store was closing for the day. I'd offer to haul away anything that was going to be tossed out. Many fine, only slightly broken watermelons and only lightly dappled apples made their way into my little red wagon. With a bit of deft surgery, they became every bit as good as the produce selling at full price.

A variation on this theme brings us into the big time. Start haunting the major wholesale produce markets in larger towns and cities. Often you can get whole crates of unsold, slightly over-ripe fruits and vegetables for free or a fraction of their original wholesale price, which is low to begin with. Not too long ago I picked

up a big crate of tangelos (like oranges only larger) which were considered defective because they were dark-skinned (the taste was unaffected). The cost? The labor it took to get them into my car's trunk.

Ranches, Farms, and Roadside Stands

Combine a delightful picnic or nature-study trip with a good-food hunting expedition. You'll enjoy yourself, you'll save money, and you'll drive home with a car full of the freshest food possible. Roadside stands provide the easiest, most convenient access to farm-fresh produce. But many farms don't have stands, yet are still interested in making cash sales. So don't hesitate to drive into a likely looking orchard or field. Barter a bit with the owner and you may end up with a trunk full of off-the-stalk corn or ripe-from-the-tree peaches.

Another way to find rural food bargains is to buy the local town or county paper, often a weekly with items like the ones shown here.

What if you buy too much? Simply refer to Chapter 7 and learn how to preserve the surplus. Or barter the extra apples for staples at your natural food store.

Or just be generous; share your largesse with the less fortunate. Incidentally, as you will note in the ad, some farmers are willing to let you pick your own and charge accordingly, usually very little. If you've never done this, you have a most pleasant experience in store. You can make it an impromptu party amidst the trees. And remember, the few fruits you eat don't get counted (but don't worry, the farmer makes allowances for picker

consumption). Once you try it, you'll find that no plum, peach, apricot or cherry ever tasted as good as the one you picked yourself. The fruit will be sun-warm and fully ripe. Plucking them from a leafy tree in some verdant orchard on a beautiful afternoon in late August will stay in your memory and draw you back year after year.

I've really just begun here to hint at the opportunities for acquiring your food in alternative stores and rural regions. There are fish farms, dairies, cheese factories, dried-fruit barns, smokehouses, vineyards and many other food-preparation facilities dotted throughout the U.S. countryside. Many sell to travelers as part of their regular business. Others can be persuaded to part with a crate of peaches, a wheel of cheese, or a fine smoked ham for money or the right barter item. So think of this brief review as a beginner's guide. Take it from here yourself.

How to develop your bargaining skills

What you'll learn:
That you can take advantage of the
law of supply and demand, even to the
extent of naming your own price.

It's a well-known and lamentable fact that hundreds of tons of perfectly good food are thrown away each *day* in the United States simply because we are a rich nation (at least at this time) and care little for the losses that accrue from this wasteful practice. But you can take advantage of the general wastefulness by becoming a weekend warrior, mounting regular attacks on the bargain counters.

Don't try this if you're the fussy type (and I don't think you are or you wouldn't be reading this book). Keep an open mind and a ready purse; you never know when you'll spot a bargain. Don't hesitate to buy too much at one time; you can use surplus foods to barter for other things with your neighbors or with other merchants. Also, modern techniques of preserving allow you to store perishables for long periods of time (see Chapter 7).

Try these bargain-hunting techniques the next time you go shopping. Simply follow the rule that prices are determined by the law of supply and demand. Concentrate on items that are in great supply but have little demand, and learn to be in the right place at the right time.

Bargaining for Produce

If you live near a food market that closes on Sunday, drop in and have a chat with the manager some late Saturday evening just before closing. Tell him that you are a regular customer and that you are interested in helping him by buying items that are not up to selling standards but which are still edible and wholesome. For example, it's hard to sell an apple that has a worm hole or soft spot in it. Such items are usually left at the end of the week's sale. No one wants them when a perfect apple is available for the same price. But there's nothing wrong with an apple of this type that a paring knife can't cure in about two seconds. Cut out the worm hole or soft spot and the apple is as perfect as one selling for full price. The same is true of cantaloupes, watermelons, avocados, or pears that have an overripe spot. Simply cut around the spot and eat all the rest.

In the case of vegetables, make sure that despite the damaged spot the produce is still fairly fresh. Old, limp, tired and wilted vegetables have lost so much of their vitamins that they are simply not worth buying. Winter vegetables such as cabbages, cauliflower, beets, turnips, rutabagas, potatoes, and onions are not quite as delicate as other vegetables, though. These have a somewhat longer life and will store fairly well if kept in a cool dry place.

So, if you come across some damaged but still fairly fresh-appearing fruits or vegetables at your neighborhood market, your task is to buy them for as little as you can. Remember that the grocer doesn't necessarily waste this food; he takes it home and eats it himself. He is not about to give it away if he can sell it. But when stocks are plentiful, the chances are he will be willing to sell for very little. This is where your bargaining abilities can be put to good use. It's quite certain that you and the grocer can come to an agreement on a fair price for items that must be sold for cash immediately. Once you have established rapport, it will be simple for you to do most of your fruit and vegetable shopping at the end of the week. If you should latch onto a whole lug box of soft peaches, make peach jam. If you come across some overripe tomatoes, boil until tender and chuck them into your blender for instant tomato sauce, then freeze or bottle. Perhaps you can acquire a large quantity of oranges with dry, hard skins. These are hard to sell, but they're great for juice. Squeeze them and freeze the juice you can't drink immediately.

Once you've developed your bargaining skills,

start using your imagination. Consider any business that deals in good food fair game. Harry and David, for instance, is the firm that started the Fruit of the Month Club. Based in Medford, Oregon, they send gift packages of fresh fruits to all parts of the world. Their high-quality gift boxes contain only the most perfect specimens of the superlative fruit grown in their orchards. Thus, after their seasonal packaging of such items as peaches and pears, you can visit their plant at Medford and purchase large bags of what they term "rejects" for very little money. Actually, their "rejects" would outshine the best fruit in many high-class markets, since many pears are rejected, for instance, only because they are too big to conform to the standards set for gift packages.

Check around your own city and the surrounding countryside to see if there isn't a dairy, chicken farm, potato processor, or other food-handling facility that would be willing to sell you their off-standard items at a low price. Almost any egg farm, for example, keeps what they call their "checks"—slightly cracked eggs —and will sell them for far less than perfects. These are even fresher than the freshest eggs you buy in the market. Tape them up if necessary and take them home.

Variations on the Theme

This bargaining technique can be applied to many other types of stores: bakeries, meat markets, fish and seafood shops and dairies. Many bakeries, for example, will not hold products over a weekend. If you approach the baker late on Saturday, you may find an opportunity to stock your freezer with low-cost baked goods for perhaps half their regular retail price. The same holds true for meat markets, which are coming under stricter control regarding the selling of older meat. Unless the meat is actually spoiled, the darkening that is caused by too much exposure to light in the display case does not affect the wholesomeness and nutritional value. Still, many buyers pass up everything except blood-red, fresh-cut beef, so there is usually quite a bit of nourishing meat to discuss with your butcher on Saturday evening.

Fish and seafood shops are especially vulnerable

Robert Altman

to sharp bargainers. Fish has notoriously poor keeping qualities. Thus, you might make an agreement with your local fish merchant to take anything off his hands that is approaching unsalability. What can you do with a fish that will only last another day? Well, you can cut it up and freeze it, make it into a bouillabaise and freeze that, or smoke and save it for an almost indefinite time in your refrigerator.

Dents and Spills

Have you ever ventured into the back room of a grocery store? If so, you've seen bags and cartons piled to the ceiling. Frequently, these heavy storage containers fall over, spilling, damaging and denting the canned goods inside. The employees and the boss can only take some of these damaged items home for their own use. The rest is classed as "dented goods"; it is perfectly good food but cannot be sold as top-line merchandise. This is another opportunity to cut your budget substantially while you enjoy top-brand canned food. First, introduce yourself to the manager of the staple-food department of your local market. Tell him that you are a low-budget operator and would be interested in buying all types of food at discount that would normally be unsalable to the general public. You're not looking for things that are inedible, just imperfect packages. A typical example would be a dented can of fruit or soup. The contents will be undamaged as long as the can is still tightly sealed.

You can buy these "dents" for a substantial percentage off the regular price. Add these percentages up throughout the year and you'll see that they will bring your food expenditures down considerably. Let's say you have been spending a thousand dollars a year on food. If you can save just twenty-five percent, you'll have a fat $250 to play with or use for more important things. You can always use the savings to buy the delicacies that will make your diet more enjoyable. Treat yourself well; subscribe to the philosophy that you can always afford the luxuries if you save on the necessities.

Incidentally, you might make even greater savings by offering to buy all of the grocer's unsalable merchandise at once. Bidding on a pile of crumpled boxes, torn sacks, and unlabeled cans might not sound like much, but it can be an exciting and profitable event. By becoming a skillfull bargainer you can bring home a considerable supply of food for a fraction of its usual selling price.

A Word of Caution

Don't get carried away with buying up those bargain canned goods. Remember that the main consideration in the economy of food-buying lies in purchasing foods with the highest possible nutritional content. The object is eating to stay healthy, not simply eating enough to fill the stomach. Since the canning process robs foods of some of their vitamins, limit your use of canned goods to emergencies or to supplementing fresh meats and vegetables for variety. Canned foods do have their place. I'd certainly hate to tackle a spaghetti recipe without those handy little cans of tomato sauce. But I'd also hate to sit down to a meal of canned corn and beans when those vegetables were available fresh from the fields.

Bargaining for Fresh Foods

Be on the lookout for a farmer, rancher, or truck gardener who could use some help. Offer to provide labor in exchange for fresh-pulled carrots, beets, cabbages, and lettuce. My wife Ruth wrote this to me recently: "Helped Ms. Webb pick a lug of cukes for a customer and she gave me plums, apples, squash, cukes and a gallon of milk." While you'd be lucky to run into a cornucopia like that, the thought is worth keeping in mind whenever you're out for a drive.

Where to pick fresh foods for free

What You'll Learn:
How to find the thousands of
sources of free foods throughout the
United States.

A sparkling day, a melodious brook, trees festooned with climbing flowers—a perfect time for a picnic. Perhaps on such a day you discovered foods that you could have for the picking. It may have been watercress, the crisp, tart plant that grows wild in many streams. Or it may have been the sweet wild blackberries that grow in such abundance in many parts of the country. It could have been the black walnut that grows wild and produces some of the tastiest nut tidbits in the world. These are just three of the thousands of wild foods that you can gather up free of cost. The world is still full of good things to eat; it's a matter of keeping your eyes open.

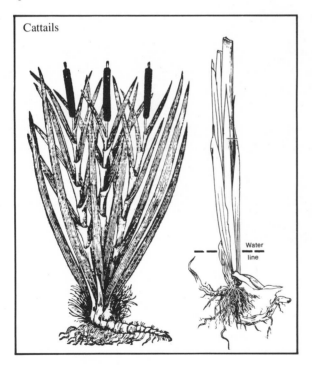

Cattails

Water line

Cattails

This prolific plant, which grows in most swamp and marsh areas of the world, is a treasure trove of delicious tidbits. I discovered this for myself one afternoon in the Santa Ynez river valley behind Santa Barbara. I had been swimming in a wonderful swimming hole, a place where the river slowed, widened, and deepened beneath a rocky bluff. On the opposite side, a gently sloping sandy beach was partly covered by a thick growth of cattails—tall, green, and lush. While swimming underwater, I could see white tendrils growing out of the cattail roots. I snapped off a couple and, willing to try anything once, surfaced and ate them. Wonderful! They tasted like the tenderest hearts of celery I'd ever had. That day I ate almost every cattail tendril I could find. I felt as though I had made a great discovery. What I didn't know was that the Chumash Indians, who once lived in that region, thought that cattail tendrils were just about as basic as the acorns they also used as a staple.

Later, when I read books on survival and life in the wilderness, I discovered that almost all parts of the cattail are useful—from the tendrils to the seed pod. The roots are the most basic edible part of the plant. Next in importance are the new shoots; you'll find these in abundance. Peel and eat them as you would fresh tender celery. Finally, try the yellow pollen produced by the seed pods. It can be used as flour if you gather enough, or added to soups, stews, cereals or anything you wish for bulk and nutrition.

The homely but tasty Cactus

Stands of thorny cactus abound in the western deserts and desert rims. They look unapproachable, but the common, broad-leafed cactus is eaten by thousands of people daily. Almost all the other North American cacti are edible and can be sliced and fried, boiled, roasted, or added to stews and soups.

Here's the procedure. Wear gloves and use a large knife or machete to cut off slabs of cactus leaves. Then fill a tub or bucket with water. Submerge the cactus and using a small paring knife dig out the clusters of sharp spines. These will float to the surface where they can be skimmed off. The spines can also be burned off over a gas flame or campfire.

Just for fun, here's one recipe. It should trigger your imagination and encourage you to experiment.

NOPALES, BASIC PREPARATION

After you make sure all the prickly spines are removed, cut the cactus leaves into cubes. Boil in slightly salted water until tender. Eat with butter, salt and pepper as a vegetable, chill and add to salads, or pickle. Any way you try them, they're not only good, they're free!

Smell them first, then eat them

I'm talking about wild roses. They are an excellent source of Vitamin C and it's yours for the taking. The vitamin is contained in the buds, or "rose hips," of wild and domestic roses. These edible goodies are the red-orange, smooth-skinned berries that grow at the end of the rose stem. They taste a little like apples (to which they are related). You can gather them to eat on the trail or take them home and prepare them in a number of ways. They can actually be used as if they were small apples. Incidentally, in Scandinavian countries rose hips are dried and powdered. The powder is used in fruit soups and hot or cold drinks, on cereals, and wherever else a sweet, nutritious powdered substance is called for. Here's a good way to put rose hips to work for you.

ROSE HIP JAM

Cut the rose hips in half and remove the seeds. Chop or grind the hips and add four cups to about 2 cups of water. Boil for about ½ hour. Then add as much raw sugar or honey as you wish and continue boiling until it reaches the desired thickness. Somewhere along the way, remove some and use it as rose hip syrup on pancakes, waffles, and biscuits. When the jam is thick, remove from fire, pour into sterilized jars, and seal in the conventional way. If you wish, add a little cinnamon or lemon juice for more flavor.

Piñon Nuts

These tasty and nutritious nuts are found in the

Melon cactus

Wild rose

cones of the piñon tree, a short, gnarled pine of the southwest. Gathering them can be fun if you make sure to take some solvent along to dissolve the sticky sap that accompanies the cone.

Piñon nuts are sold in many places as alternatives to peanuts though their flavor is really more delicate. Piñon nuts can also be ground into flour. Removed from their soft shell and pounded, they become a wonderful addition to pancake batter, cookies, or other baked goods. Try sprinkling a few shelled nuts on top of plain cookies.

Birch Tea

Birch trees abound in North America. Most people remember their tall beauty and some know that the bark can be used as canoe material. But few people are aware that birches can provide a most refreshing tea. Just gather young leaves, bark, and the soft new growth between the wood and bark. Chop it up and boil it in water. It becomes a most delicious beverage with a flavor similar to that of wintergreen tea.

Birches have other uses too. The young, tender, inner bark can be eaten raw, cut into strips and added to stews or soups, or dried and carried for munching on the trail. The sap of birches can be gathered and boiled for use as a delicately flavored syrup. Drill a small hole in the tree in spring or early summer when the sap is flowing best. Hang a small tin can or cup beneath the hole and go on to the next tree while the first one drips. When you've collected a substantial amount of sap, boil it until it reaches the desired thickness, add a speck of cinnamon or other spice, and you have an unusually tasty syrup for just the fun of making it.

Blackberries

Of all the berries that grow wild in the North American continent, none is so sweet, so lush, and so easy to find as the blackberry. Bushes of these luscious treats grow alongside roads and byways in many states. In terms of time expended, little compares with the returns from a berry-picking expedition. Besides the obvious and instant pleasure of eating them right off the bush, there are dozens of ways to make wild blackberries a part of your gourmet diet. Here are just a few:

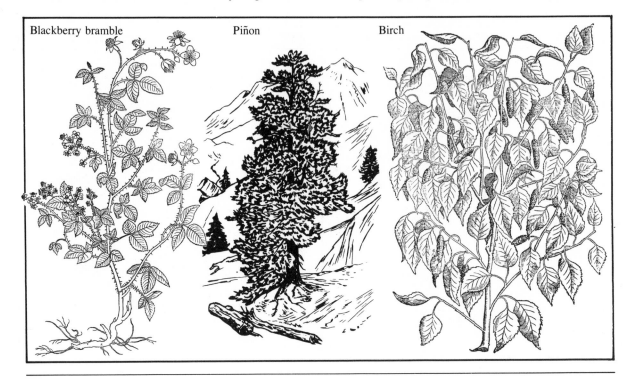

Blackberry bramble   Piñon   Birch

BLACKBERRY SLUMP (COBBLER)

May be made with any fruit—peaches for example.

4 cups blackberries
½ cup honey (optional if berries are sweet enough for your taste)
4 tablespoons cornstarch
1 teaspoon nutmeg

Bring these slowly to a boil in a heavy saucepan. While the mixture is simmering, make a batter of:

2 tablespoons honey
3 tablespoons shortening
½ cup milk
1½ cups sifted whole wheat flour
1½ teaspoons baking powder

Cream honey and shortening. Add the milk and mix thoroughly. Sift the flour and baking powder together. Stir rapidly into the other ingredients. Then begin dropping the batter, spoonful by spoonful, over the bubbling berries. Cover and cook at the same speed for 10 minutes. Serve hot with cream. Cost: 45 cents.

BLACKBERRY PIE

This pie isn't solid with thickeners such as arrowroot, tapioca, or cornstarch, so it won't hold together while you punctuate your conversation with the occasional forkful. As a matter of fact, most backwoodsmen who sit down to this particular dessert are glad to hold up on the repartee for a while and finish off with a spoon.

All you need besides the pastry is 4 cups of fresh blackberries, ½ cup honey, and ¾ cup melted butter. As for the cooking, it just takes a single operation.

Line a well-greased pie pan with pastry. Mix the berries, honey, and butter. Pour them into the uncooked shell. Top with the upper crust, making sure to cut vents. Bake in a preheated oven at 375° for about 50 minutes or until the crust is golden brown. Cost: 55 cents.

BLACKBERRY JAM

Boil together for 5 minutes: 4 cups of blackberries, 1 cup honey, and 1 teaspoon mixed cloves, cinnamon, and nutmeg. Remove from heat and add a bottle of commercial pectin. Skim, pour into sterile jars, seal, label, and store. Cost: 44 cents.

Acorns

Acorns were once a staple of many Indian groups, and are still eaten in many parts of the world. These oak nuts are nutritious and tasty. All they need is a

Bill Kaysing

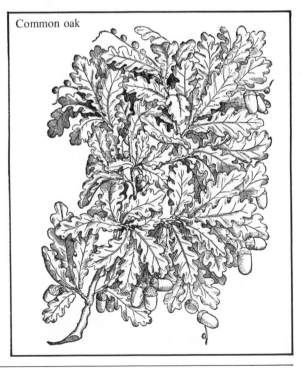

Common oak

Foraged Foods

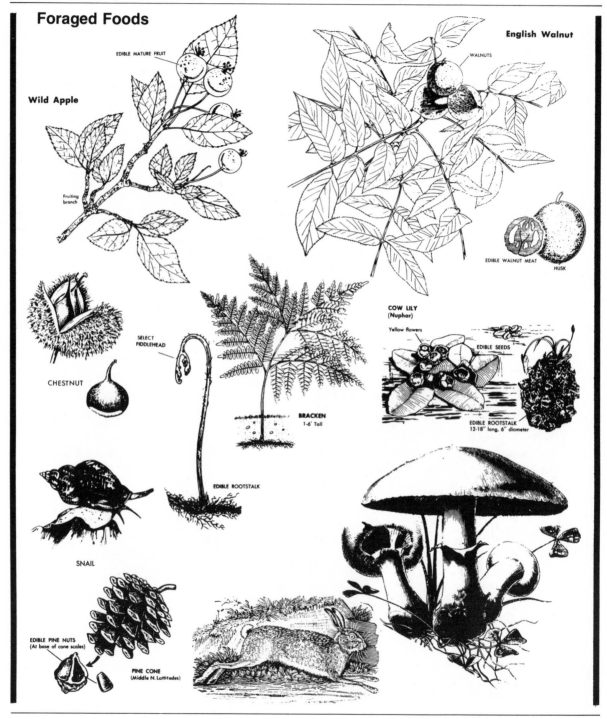

Wild Apple

EDIBLE MATURE FRUIT

Fruiting branch

English Walnut

WALNUTS

EDIBLE WALNUT MEAT

HUSK

CHESTNUT

SELECT FIDDLEHEAD

BRACKEN
1-6' Tall

EDIBLE ROOTSTALK

COW LILY
(Nuphar)

Yellow flowers

EDIBLE SEEDS

EDIBLE ROOTSTALK
12-18" long, 6" diameter

SNAIL

EDIBLE PINE NUTS
(At base of cone scales)

PINE CONE
(Middle N. Latitudes)

preliminary treatment to remove tannin. Just grind them up and leach the tannin out with several changes of hot water. Or simply boil them for a while, then dry and grind them into flour. Use as you would any coarse whole wheat flour. Indians made cakes similar to pancakes or tortillas from acorn flour.

Olives

Las Vegas, Nevada would probably be the last place you would think to look for wild or free food. But down the street from where I'm writing these words dozens of olive trees are thriving. At this time of year, late fall, they are laden with hundreds of pounds of ripening olives, and no one seems to want the fruit, including the owners of the trees. The olives drop to the ground on the neighborhood lawns and rot. Some enterprising soul could make it a seasonal habit to knock on doors and get permission to pick the olives. After all, olives are one of the few fruits or vegetables that produce a large quantity of usable oil.

* Write to the Superintendent of Documents, U.S. Government Printing Office, Washington, D.C. 20402 for availability and current price.

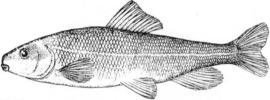

Fishing

Many astute food gatherers carry a small, compact fishing pole or drop line in their cars or jacket pockets. It's a good habit to develop. Whenever you spot a likely place to drop a line, do it. A fat, fresh fish might grace your frying pan that very evening. A small slingshot or small air pistol can serve to bag you some small animals.

This chapter has only scratched the surface of what's available to you practically in your own back yard. The U.S. Army *Survival Guide** notes that 300,000 plants grow on our planet, and that over 100,000 are edible. So expand your food horizons; not all of what you eat need come from a store. And think of the outdoor exercise you'll get while toting your market basket through wood and glade!

This is a small sampling of the thousands of wild foods that you can gather up free of cost.

Wild olive

Your kitchen is your workshop

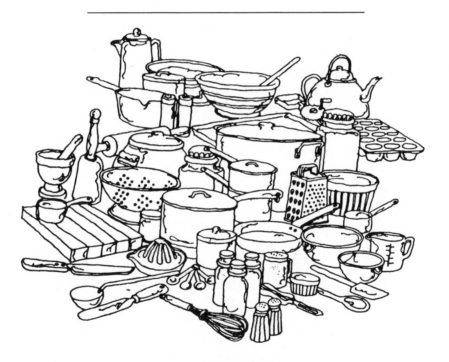

What You'll Learn:
How the right tools can make
cooking for you and your family a great
pleasure.

You really need very few items to set up a basic working kitchen: a convenient place to chop and cut, a pot, a pan, a good knife, a wooden spoon perhaps, and a pancake turner. A strainer is handy too. Remember what great food you can make in the wilds with nothing but a few green sticks and some knowhow. Buy your kitchen utensils as you find them at flea markets, the Salvation Army, or garage sales. And restaurant-supply houses are great places to browse in when you're out to stock your kitchen. To get you thinking, a ridiculously overstocked kitchen inventory is given opposite. No one needs all this junk, but it will let you know what's available.

You'll determine your needs based on this list depending on how much you like tools for their own sake and how well you can adapt one tool to a variety of purposes. Now on to the more exotic possibilities.

The Fireless Cooker

When I was a small boy, my father often took me to barbecues sponsored by his company. These were Spanish-style outings where whole sides of beef would be placed over glowing coals in a huge pit, covered tightly, and allowed to mellow slowly throughout the long day. I've never forgotten the taste of those tender, succulent morsels of beef, and I've never been able to describe it. Often, beans and potatoes were cooked in

---

Basic Necessities

Pans
 1-quart with lid
 3-quart with lid
 2- or 3-quart double
  boiler
Skillets (preferably iron)
 6″ with lid
 10″ with lid
Kettles
 6-quart with lid
Baking pans
 6-quart dutch oven
 15″ pan
 13 × 9 × 2″ loaf pan
 9 × 5 × 3″ bread pan
  (several)
 2 cookie sheets

Casseroles and Bowls
 2-quart casserole with
  lid
 nest of mixing bowls
Measurers
 measuring spoon cluster
 2 4-cup liquid measur-
  ing cups
 graduated dry measur-
  ing cup cluster
Thermometers
 meat, deep fat, and
  oven
Cutlery
 2 paring knives
 all-purpose medium-
  size knife
 large slicing knife
 vegetable peeler

cleavers, one small, one
 large
grater
food grinder
kitchen shears
sharpening stone or
 knife sharpener
Other utensils
 wooden spoons, as-
  sorted sizes and shapes
 ladle
 cooking fork
 strainer
 funnel
 pancake turner
 egg beater
 fruit juicer
 corkscrew
 can and bottle opener

the pit too, and they were equally delicious. You can achieve these ambrosial results in your own home; all you need to do is build yourself a simple fireless cooker.

The fireless cooker consists of a cooking pot tightly sealed within an insulated box. Start with a dutch oven, the heavy cast iron type, and find a large pasteboard, wooden, or metal box big enough to contain it. Place lots of crumpled newspapers in the bottom of the box, put the oven on them and then tightly pack newspapers all around the sides to fill the remaining space in the box. It's that simple, although you might want to add a few personal refinements. Professionally built fireless cookers consist of smooth-sided tubes into which the cooking pot fits. They also have handy lids to seal off the pot. But the homemade version works on the same principle. All you're really after is a cooking container that retains its own heat.

To use the cooker, merely put the meat, beans, or whatever you are going to cook in the pot with all spices, water, and vegetables. Cover and bring to a boil on your regular stove. Then place the whole works in the insulated box, seal it up, and leave it for about eight hours. You can actually leave it overnight or for the day when you're going out and about. When you open the box you'll find that your meal has been cooked slowly in its own juices by the stored heat. What a grand meal to come home to!

The Blender

My wife says if she had to give up all her small appliances, her blender would be the last to go. She uses it for almost every meal. She throws in the dried-out crusts of bread that accumulate to make bread crumbs. For nourishing drinks she tosses in any variety of fruit—an apple, a slightly overripe banana or peach, some leftover strawberries. To this she adds some skim milk, a bit of honey for sweetening, a raw egg yolk for protein, some wheat germ, and voila! a complete and delicious lunch. An economical and swiftly made salad dressing will consist of some buttermilk, yogurt, mayonnaise and a hunk of blue cheese—a difficult mixture to make by hand but easy in the blender. And speaking of mayonnaise, we make our own in the blender and like it far better than any commercial variety. If you buy oil in bulk quantities, homemade

Fireless cookers

OUTSIDE LID
PAPER STUFFED CUSHION 7.5 CM. THICK
WELL LID
COOKING POT WITH LID
HEATING STONE WIRE HANDLE CAST IN CONCRETE
WELL WITH 2.5 CM. SAND IN THE BOTTOM
OUTSIDE CONTAINER
OILCLOTH COVERED CARDBOARD COLLAR
SHREDDED NEWSPAPER 7.5 CM THICK
10 CM. HIGH ROLLS OF NEWSPAPER PACKED IN BOTTOM

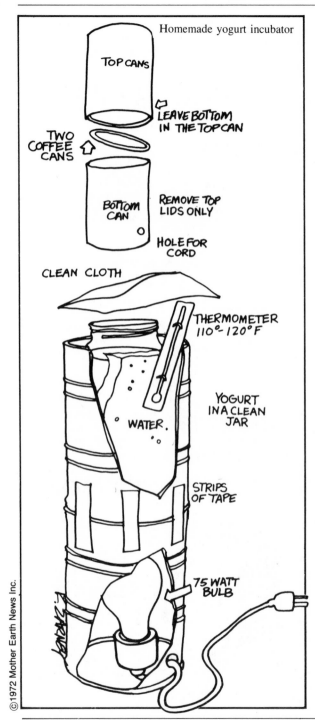

Homemade yogurt incubator

TOP CANS

LEAVE BOTTOM IN THE TOP CAN

TWO COFFEE CANS

BOTTOM CAN   REMOVE TOP LIDS ONLY

HOLE FOR CORD

CLEAN CLOTH

THERMOMETER 110°-120°F

YOGURT IN A CLEAN JAR

WATER.

STRIPS OF TAPE

75 WATT BULB

mayonnaise costs far less than commercial brands.

The Yogurt Maker

If you're a yogurt enthusiast you may consider buying a yogurt maker, or you may be satisfied with a home-built set-up. The commercial yogurt maker consists mainly of a heat source and comes with its own jars, but you can get away with as little as one large jar as long as you can set it in a place which will give it some steady warmth. You can place the jar over the pilot on your stove or on a heating pad. Or perhaps you have a warm closet that houses the hot water heater.

Yogurt is one of those dishes that fits in anywhere. It's a meal in itself for those who prefer a light lunch, and a luxurious dessert for dinner if it's mixed with naturally sweet fruit. And so easy to make:

YOGURT

Mix 1 cup whole milk, 2 tablespoons commercial yogurt or yogurt from your last homemade batch, 1 cup non-instant milk powder, 3 cups warm water. Shake or blend. Pour mixture into small bowls and keep at about 110° F for 3 to 8 hours until set. When thick refrigerate. Flavor to suit with anything you like, from cinnamon to chopped fruits.

Chinese Items: Cleavers and Woks

The next time you go to a Chinese restaurant ask the proprietor to let you tour the kitchen. There you'll see the Chinese secret to simple, efficient food preparation. There will be a sturdy chopping block, one end of which empties onto a work table, the other into a waste receptacle. Arranged nearby will be an assortment of high-carbon steel cleavers with edges like razors. These relatively heavy cutting instruments make the chopping, slicing, dicing, and trimming of vegetables a pleasure. Try it yourself and see. The cleaver does all the work; you just raise it and lower it and keep your fingers out of the way. Once you're familiar with the cleaver, you won't want to go back to an ordinary knife. Since the Chinese use large quantities of vegetables in their cooking, it's understandable that they settled on a sturdy block and cleaver many centuries ago. If you have vegetarian leanings, you'll want to use that combination too.

The basic Chinese cooking utensil is the wok. It's a very simple, shallow metal bowl with sloping sides. Food is cooked at the center of the wok balanced over the heat source. Very little heat is required to cook foods in this way, an important consideration in fuel-poor areas of rural China and in energy-conscious American cities. Also, the edges of the wok retain heat, keeping the cooked, ready-to-serve foods warm once they leave the stove.

You'll find cleavers and woks in any Chinatown supply store. Or, if you're far from metropolitan areas, write to the Chamber of Commerce in your closest major city and ask for up-to-date listings of suppliers.

From Wok to Crock

A large ceramic crock holding five gallons or more will be a valuable addition to your kitchen equipment. Heavy, durable, and big enough to stay put when you stir things in it, this container can be used in many ways. For example, it's the perfect place to mix your bread dough and let it rise. It's great for making batches of fruit drinks. And you can crush grapes or other fruits or do your pickling in it. When not in use for mixing, a crock is a fine place to store bulk foods.

The Witch's Cauldron

A companion to the ceramic crock is a big substan-tial pot. Restaurant kitchens, you'll find, always have a huge pot simmering on the back of the stove full of stock for soups, gravy, or sauce. You'll need an over-sized pot in which to make large quantities of chili beans, spaghetti sauce, chowder, or beef stew. Made at one time in quantity, these foods can be divided into meal-sized portions and frozen. Cooking in large quantities is one of the keys to cutting food costs.

The Tenderizer and The Masher

Among the smaller kitchen tools you'll need are the meat tenderizer (a hammer with a diamond pattern on its pounding surface), and a business-like potato masher. The latter is great for preparing the many dishes where reduction of ingredients to fine particles is essential.

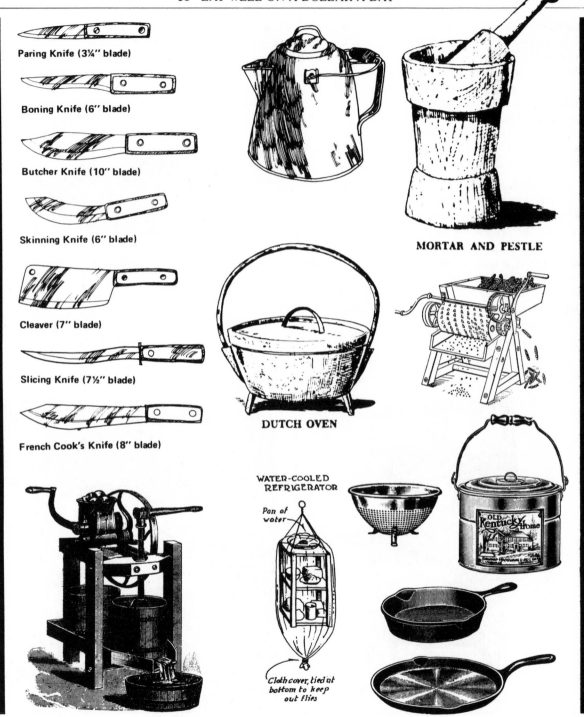

Paring Knife (3¼" blade)

Boning Knife (6" blade)

Butcher Knife (10" blade)

Skinning Knife (6" blade)

Cleaver (7" blade)

Slicing Knife (7½" blade)

French Cook's Knife (8" blade)

MORTAR AND PESTLE

DUTCH OVEN

WATER-COOLED REFRIGERATOR

Pan of water

Cloth cover, tied at bottom to keep out flies

Coffee and Meat Grinders

Meat grinders are used for making sausage, grinding tough meats for use in soups and fillings, and sometimes shredding vegetables. Coffee grinders are useful for many foods besides coffee: use one to make bean flour, blend dry ingredients when even distribution is essential, grind nuts into a flavorful powder, etc. You can often find grinders in antique stores, second-hand shops, and flea markets.

To use the grinder efficiently, find a space on a sturdy bench, table, or sideboard where you can clamp it semi-permanently. Then it will always be ready when you need it.

Grain Grinders

Grain grinders are even more essential to the budget-conscious cook, but they are just as important in terms of nutrition. The old stone and flour mills our forefathers used produced flours and meal that retained all the important elements of each grain of wheat and each kernel of corn, including the vital germ oils. There was no heat problem during milling to cause the food to turn rancid and spoil, and there were no pro-

cessing problems resulting in large losses of vital nutrients. With all the nourishing and tasty elements of the grain intact, breads, biscuits, pies, cakes, and other baked goods tasted great and were positive additions to a healthy diet. You can produce the same results straight from your pantry if you own your own hand- or motor-driven grain and flour mill. Many varieties are on the market. As an added bonus, you'll save a great deal of money in grinding your own flour. After all, when you buy packaged flour and meal, all you're really paying for is the labor and packaging.

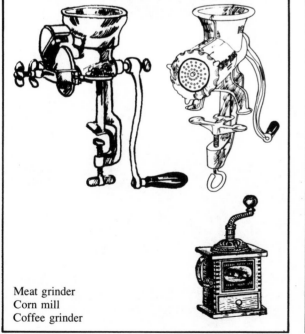

Meat grinder
Corn mill
Coffee grinder

Food you can
grow yourself

What You'll Learn:
Priced out of the produce market?
Even if you don't have land, you can
learn to grow fruits and vegetables in
pots, tubs, and planters.

Here are a few quotations from a vegetable seed catalogue:

Mary Washington Asparagus: One ounce produces *600* roots. Cost per ounce: 50 cents. (Have you priced a can of asparagus lately?)

Danvers Half Long Carrot: One ounce will plant a 300 foot row. Cost per ounce: 95 cents. (At this price you could feed them to your pig!)

Savor Cabbage: 7,000 seeds per ounce. Cost per ounce: 95 cents. (Hmmm, let's see. 7,000 heads of cabbage at 15 cents each is . . .)

Bronze Lettuce: ¼ ounce plants a hundred foot row. Cost per ounce: 85 cents. (Made into salads they would fill a child's swimming pool.)

These quotes are intended to show you just how much you can add to your diet for little or no money. All you have to do is cultivate the soil and add the water and some exhilarating work; the bounty-bringing sun does all the rest.

Space

If you have room around your house for a half-acre garden (100 feet by 200 feet), it's enough to grow *all* the vegetables and small fruits that a *large* family can eat with *plenty left over* for canning, preserving, drying, or selling to others.

PRICES:

Tomatoes	*12 to 29*
Corn	*5 to 10*
Musk melon, etc.	*13-15/lb.*
Strawberries	*25-29/basket*
Raspberries	*60/basket*
Asparagus	*39-59/lb.*

Seeds

It pays to buy the best seeds from a reputable seed firm. The cost involved is usually so small that it would be a false economy to use anything but the best. Here are a few of the many reputable seed firms in the U.S. For more addresses, consult some of the gardening magazines:

W. Atlee Burpee Company, 4061 Burpee Building, Philadelphia, Pennsylvania 19132; (Exceptionally fine catalog!)

Burrell Seed Company, Box 150-G, Rocky Ford, Colorado 81067.

Farmer Seed and Nursery Company, Ellicott Street Station, Buffalo, New York 14205.

Girard Nurseries, Geneva, Ohio 44041.

Gurney Seed and Nursery Company, 2642 Page Street, Yankton, South Dakota 57077; (Splashy, colorful, delightful!)

Joseph Harris Company, Inc., 48 Moreton Farm, Rochester, New York 14624; (Very professional. Quantity wholesale prices).

Harry E. Saier, Dimondale, Michigan 48821. ($.50).

Hemlock Hill Herb Farms, Litchfield, Connecticut 06759.

Henry Field, Shenandoah, Iowa 51601.

J. W. Jung Seed Company, Station 23, Randolph, Wisconsin 53956.

Mellingers, North Lima, Ohio 44452; (Dozens of unique items).

Natural Development Company, Bainbridge, Pennsylvania 17502.

Nichols Garden Nursery, 1190 N. Pacific Highway, Albany, Oregon 93721; (Strong on herbs and oddities—entertaining).

Opposite; top: Figure A. Typical Garden Plan, 160 x 270 feet. Center: The 15 x 60 foot plot, divided in two for convenient rotation of crops.

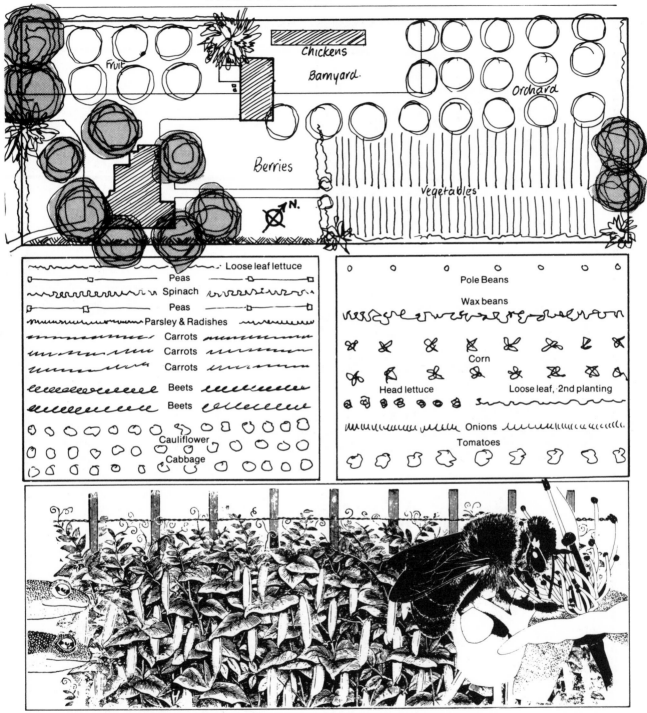

Fruit

Chickens

Barnyard.

Orchard

Berries

Vegetables

N.

Loose leaf lettuce
Peas
Spinach
Peas
Parsley & Radishes
Carrots
Carrots
Carrots
Beets
Beets
Cauliflower
Cabbage

Pole Beans
Wax beans
Corn
Head lettuce   Loose leaf, 2nd planting
Onions
Tomatoes

Grow Your Own Seedlings:

1. *Sprinkle seeds into furrows, cover lightly and water.*
2. *Nature takes care of germination.*

3. *A well-sprouted seedling bed ready for transplanting.*
4. *Cut individual plants apart just like a one-layer cake.*

5. *Transplant to prepared rows outdoors . . .*
6. *. . . then protect with homemade shields.*

Crate top

½ milk carton

Cardboard

Shingle

Parks Seed Company, Inc., Greenwood, South Carolina 29646.

Robson Quality Seeds, Inc., 18 Hall, New York, New York 14463.

Stark Bros., Louisiana, Missouri 63353.

Stokes Seeds, Inc., Box 15, Ellicott Street Station, Buffalo, New York 14205.

Tennessee Nursery Company, P.O. 111, Cleveland, Tennessee 37311.

Vita Green Farms, P.O. 878, Vista, California 92083.

Soil and Seedlings

As anyone who has grown any plant knows, the constitution of the soil is of prime importance. It must contain the nutrients needed by the plant or else nothing happens. Rich soil produces lush plants. Here's an easy way to learn about your soil and to prepare your own mix for a seedling garden (see Figure B). Procure a wooden lug box and place newspapers or cardboard over the holes to prevent the dirt from falling through but still permit drainage. Next, pour in one-third clean builders sand, one-third manure or compost (the latter is simply the rotted remains of mixed vegetation) and one-third of the best top soil you can find in your neighborhood. Mix it well and dampen. Now use your finger or a stick to "plow" a series of furrows about 3 inches apart. Sprinkle your seeds into the furrow and cover lightly. Sprinkle with water once more. Place your plants-to-be in a warm corner of your home and await results. In a week or less, the green sprouts (just like your salad sprouts) should poke through the soil. When this happens move the seedling flat to the light near a window and allow the sprouts to mature. Sprinkle lightly once a day.

Transplanting

When the weather permits (no more frosts; check Figure C), you can cut up the seedling box like a one-

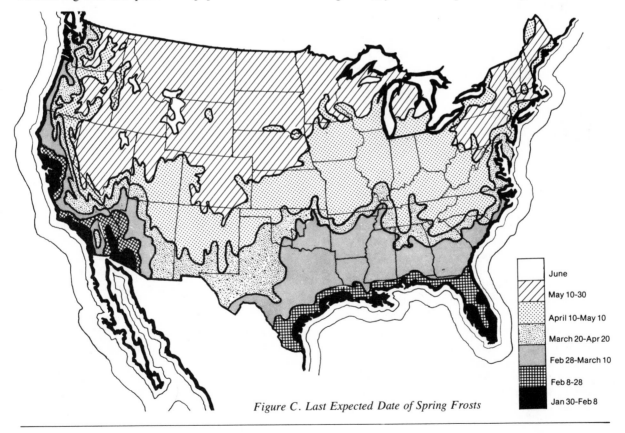

	June
	May 10-30
	April 10-May 10
	March 20-Apr 20
	Feb 28-March 10
	Feb 8-28
	Jan 30-Feb 8

Figure C. Last Expected Date of Spring Frosts

layer cake and move your seedlings outdoors. Remove as much of the original soil as possible and place the tender new plants in a well-cultivated and well-manured or composted row. Leave plenty of room between plants; if you make a mistake, make it on the side of too much rather than too little room. This is especially true of plants like squash and pumpkin, which love to roam all over creation.

Your first-time-plants will look very vulnerable in their new, outdoor home because they are. You can protect them with homemade "tents" made from milk cartons, pieces of cardboard, or old shingles.

Watering your new transplants is a matter of judgment. If they begin to look withered, add water. If the soil is muddy, hold off for a few days. Soon you'll be able to judge by plant and soil appearance the amount of water to add. It's been established by experts that frequent light waterings are far better than periodic floodings. This allows the plant to breath between inundations; air is as important to plant life as water with a few exceptions.

No Room?

Don't have an outdoors? Live in a tight little city? Then just transplant your seedlings to pots, tubs, Number 10 tin cans, window boxes, planters and raised beds. The latter is simply a much larger seedling box placed on a fire escape, roof, or wherever you have room and there's sun. There are advantages to this method of horticulture; animals such as gophers and moles usually don't live in tubs and cans. Also, you'll be able to move your plants around to take advantage of the best sun and weather protection. Further, you'll be safe from hungry neighbors who might be thinking of a midnight raid on your carrot patch.

Another solution to space problems is communal growing of vegetables and small fruits. Is there an empty lot or two in your neighborhood? If so, why not

gather a group together and find a way to use the lot for a community garden? It's being done in many areas with enthusiasm. In these times of high costs and short supply, it makes good sense to try to alleviate both problems communally and reap the benefits of outdoor exercise at the same time.

Growing

Actually, this is done by the plants themselves, not you, so there is not much to do except keep out bone-burying dogs, goats and pesky insects. A fence takes care of the first two and here are some suggestions on the latter:

1. *Phrethrum:* dried, ground flower of oriental chrysanthemum. Also known as Dalmation powder.

2. *Rotenone:* Powder from roots (tropical) containing rotenone.

3. *Soap Spray:* 2 tablespoons soap flakes (not detergents) in 1 quart water.

3a. *Nicotine Sulphate:* add 3 above. Bought as Black Leaf. Follow directions on label.

4. *Dusting Sulphur:* never use against house or fence as discolors paint.

4a. 4 above used with Pyrethrum.

5. *Water:* use as a fine strong spray, preferably in hand sprayer. Care not to flood.

6. *Mineral Oil Spray:* 3 parts oil/100 parts water.

7. *Wood Ash:* around base of plants to discourage cutworms.

8. *Epsom Salt Spray:* 2 ozs. salt, 2 gallons water.

9. *Beer:* stale or with molasses in saucer in garden.

10. *Ryanta:* root and woody stem of South American plant.

11. *Pepper:* (hot peppers in water), or Cayenne pepper. sprayed when plants wet with dew.

12. *Bordeaux Mixture:* can be bought ready mixed.

13. *Borax and Icing Sugar:* mix together in equal parts, sprinkle on ground or rocks.

14. *Tomato Leaves Spray:* crush and soak in water, strain.

15. *Rhubarb Leaves:* boil 3 lbs. leaves in 3 qts. water. Strain, add to 1 oz. soap flakes dissolved in 1 qt. water.

16. *Traps:* cutworms and millipeds come to surface at night. Use gloves and flashlight to catch them.

17. *Naphthalene:* dig into ground 2 oz/10 sq. feet.

18. *Trap for Grasshoppers and Ants:* Paraffin lined pill boxes or cans baited with sugar water, bacon rind, scraps. Drop filled traps in boiling water.

19. Encourage, buy, cultivate all bird life, ladybugs, preying mantisses, spiders, lizards, salamanders, bats and toads for truly effective pest control.

Mulching

Weeds can be a problem but mulching your new plants with straw or grass cuttings can reduce the number of unwanted volunteers. Mulching means to cover the ground except where your desired plants are growing. A six-inch thickness is not too much, though a thinner protective layer would probably do the job. See the wonderful book on the subject of mulching by Ruth Stout listed below.

Harvesting

Nutritionally, all plants have a peak of goodness. Experimentation will tell you just when to pull the carrots and pick the corn. Certainly this is the fun part of growing your own foods, the delicious payoff that makes all your efforts worthwhile.

Selected Bibliography for Gardening

Does the above sound simple, almost too easy? Well, that's because growing things for your own kitchen use really *is* simple. After all, think of the billions of tons of wild foods that plant themselves, fight off insects and marauders and produce a bountiful harvest without benefit of human intervention. That's why we recommend the casual approach to gardening—let nature do practically all the work since she knows best.

For further information, we suggest the following books from your local library or book store or direct from the publishers (addresses given).

The Sunset Garden Book, Lane Book Company, Menlo Park, California 94025.

How to Have a Green Thumb without an Aching Back, A New Method of Mulch Gardening, Ruth Stout, Exposition Press, 50 Jericho Turnpike, Jericho, New York 11753.

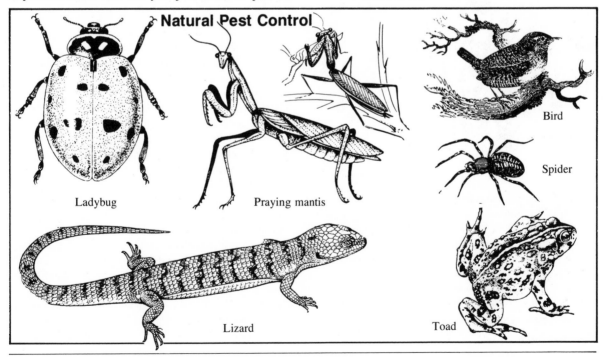

Natural Pest Control

Ladybug

Praying mantis

Bird

Spider

Lizard

Toad

The Encyclopedia of Organic Gardening, J. I. Rodale, Rodale Press, Emmaus, Pennsylvania 18049.

How to Grow Vegetables and Fruits by the Organic Method–Anyone Can Have a Green Thumb, A. D. Pardee, Hearthside Press, 381 Park Avenue South, New York 10016.

The Ex-Urbanites Complete and Illustrated Easy Does It First Time Farmers Guide, Bill Kaysing, Straight Arrow Books, 625 - 3rd St., San Francisco, California 94107.

Suburban and Farm Vegetable Gardens, U.S.D.A., Superintendent of Documents, U.S. Government Printing Office, Washington, D.C. 20402. This item is a 46-page booklet full of valuable information and cost only 30 cents at last report. Also, if you'll write the U.S.D.A. directly (Washington, D.C. 20250) and ask about problems related to your own area, they'll send you specific data. Another source is your State Department of Agriculture located in the capitol of your state.

To sum up the reasons for growing your own:

• You'll save money for sure. Since a half-acre garden will produce more than enough for a large family, the value of the crop will be about equal to your present vegetable and small-fruit budget.

• Everyone in the family will enjoy growing their own favorite vegetables and small fruits.

• Your fruits and vegetables will be fresher and more healthful. In addition, since you won't use poison sprays, you'll be cutting down on the amount of insecticides you ingest.

• If you really do have a green thumb, you can sell the surplus output of your home garden and make a profit to buy things you don't grow.

And while you're growing your basics outside, why not cultivate the trimmings inside your house.

Grow Your Own Sprouts

Sprouts!!! You can grow them fresh all year long, and right inside your kitchen at that. This is fresh food—indeed, it is growing food right up to the moment you consume it. Use sprouts raw in salads or sandwiches. Cooking them by steaming causes only a small loss in vitamin content.

Here's all you have to do. Soak a tablespoon of seeds overnight in a quart-size glass jar. Any kind of seeds can be used: alfalfa, beans (soy, mung, kidney, navy, or any other type), lentils, peas, sunflower seeds, and even wheat, oats, barley, and rye. Now place a piece of cheese cloth, nylon stocking, or other loosely woven fabric over the top of the jar and hold it in place with a rubber band or string. Next morning, pour out the water and place the jar in a warm, dark cupboard. Two or three times a day, take out the jar, pour in cool water to cover the seeds and pour it out again. This keeps the seeds moist but not wet, thus permitting them to sprout just as they would in the ground.

Alternatively, you can place your seeds on two layers of clean cloth, cover with two or more layers of clean cloth, soak the whole package, and allow to drain (placing on a tray with drainage in the bottom is ideal). Then place in a dark spot and continue rinsing and draining as with the jar method. You can also buy all sorts of expensive equipment (heavy crocks, nozzles with fine spray attachments, etc.) but the results are the same as those you'll obtain with the no-cost jars or scrap cloth.

In three or four days, more or less, you'll find that the seeds have become beautiful crunchy sprouts. Those from mung beans will look just like the ones you have enjoyed in Chinese foods. They're ready for you to gobble up for the optimum in good nutrition. You can increase their chlorophyll content by placing them in indirect sunlight for several hours. A window sill will do nicely. To use them, let your imagination run wild. Toss them in salads, mix them with any other vegetable combinations, add them to potato patties or rice dishes, or make the best sandwich imaginable with a layer of sprouts (preferably alfalfa), some sliced avocado, tomatoes, and mayonnaise.

When winter comes and fresh green vegetables are hard to come by, sprouted seeds are a great nutritional asset. They are loaded with Vitamin C and the B complex vitamins. One-half cup of soy sprouts, for instance, is equal in Vitamin C to six glasses of orange juice. In fact, sprouts contain all the known vitamins and are rich in potassium, phosphorous, and calcium. You get all of this food value by spending a few days waiting and a few pennies a pound. Let's say that you use mung beans to sprout; they sell for about 70 cents a pound. When sprouted they'll not only be far more nutritious than the original beans, they'll weigh from four to six times more than when they were dry. Thus, you'll be growing a fresh, multi-purpose vegetable in your own home for about 12 to 18 cents a pound and no waste!

The pioneers heading west drew on their sprouting experience to supplement their diet in another way. They let corn seeds become small plants and then ate the leaves. It was called corn salad and was often the only fresh food obtainable during the winter. I tried it and it works beautifully. Just buy some whole grain corn at your feed store, put it in a saucer and keep it just barely damp; the seeds will do the rest. If transplanted, the sprouting corn makes a handsome indoor plant, too.

The Window Box Herb Garden

How about watching your own fresh herbs grow? Then bang together a simple structure that looks like this:

Fill it with rich soil and plant some herbs. Chives, parsley, and rosemary are easy to grow. Place the box

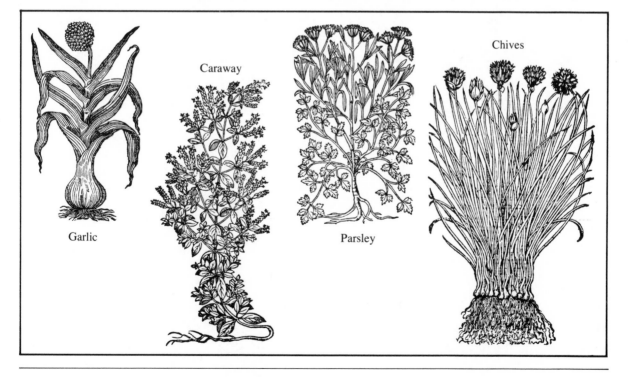

Garlic

Caraway

Parsley

Chives

Rosemary

Sage

just outside your kitchen window where the plants can enjoy the sun and you can enjoy their progress. If you live in a cold climate, set the box indoors and keep it within sight of the outdoor light. You'll have what amounts to a greenhouse in miniature.

Herbs can be grown from cuttings (mint for example) or seeds (dill) or bulbs (garlic). An excellent source of all herb materials and instructions is Nichols Nursery, Park North, Albany, Oregon 97321. See also *The Complete Book of Herbs*, K. N. Sanecki (Macmillan).

Here are some typical growing plans.

Chives can be grown from seed or from existing bulb clumps. Divide the clumps and transplant to your window box or kitchen garden. They need lots of moisture and love shade. Pick off the flowers to keep the leaves, the edible part, growing. Cut with scissors and sprinkle over salads, chili, or cottage cheese for a brisk, oniony flavor.

Dill is best grown in your garden since it is a large plant. Sprinkle seeds along one edge. Thin to 18 inches apart and keep well watered. When mature, the dried sprigs are added to pickles and such. The seeds alone make a tasty addition to many foods.

Basil is a favorite herb and grows easily and well almost anywhere. Sprinkle seeds, cover lightly and water frequently. You'll find that it grows prolifically. Great fresh or dried on and in such dishes as soy bean loaf, spaghetti sauce, scrambled eggs and sliced tomatoes.

Sage is an herb that you don't have to grow if you live in the desert regions of the American southwest. You can pick enough leaves off this grey-green bush to last you a lifetime in just one stroll through the sand and cactus. If you're not a desert dweller, grow sage from seeds by sprinkling in a corner of your garden and watering sparingly. Add the leaves to turkey stuffing, or any dish where a strong and vigorous flavor is desired. Incidentally, the favorite Italian herb, oregano, is a variety of mountain sage.

Other herbs, such as tarragon, marjoram, caraway, mint, parsley, rosemary and thyme can be grown as easily as those mentioned above. So add to the flavor of what would otherwise be plain tasting foods with the addition of fresh and dried, home-grown herbs and spices.

Watermint

Growing your own grain on unused land is always a possibility. So is communal agriculture or sharecropping. Any method is fine as long as you end up with fresh, unprocessed basic foods.

How to preserve your perishables

What You'll Learn:
A number of ways to keep foods
edible for long periods of time. These
include drying, smoking, and dry and
liquid storage.

The advantages of knowing some or all of the preserving methods is obvious. Let's say that someone presents you with a twenty-pound tuna or four five-pound barracudas. You eat what you can of the fresh fish, but what about the rest? Nothing tastes better than smoked fish, so knowing how to smoke them will not only pay off financially; you'll reap a lot of pleasure from it as well.

The same holds true for a windfall of, say, fresh apricots. Perhaps you have made arrangements to pick them in some farmer's orchard for a few cents per pound. What you cannot eat fresh, you should try to preserve. A knowledge of drying, canning, freezing or other methods will make your winter more pleasant.

Drying

The easiest way to preserve any food, from cuts of beef to apricots, is to dry it. To dry beef, for example, cut it into long strips about one-half inch thick. Then hang the strips in a dry place with plenty of sun and air circulation and protection from insects. The strips will gradually take on a hard, leathery texture creating what is known as beef jerky. This, as anyone who has done extensive camping can tell you, will keep almost indefinitely. Jerky can be eaten as is (if you have a good set of teeth) or cut up and used in stew, soup, or other dishes. As a part of a low-cost budget, it's hard to beat for economy and good taste. Keep in mind that all kinds of meat can be preserved in this manner including venison, moose, and bear. So whenever you are on the receiving end of a gift of wild game, you won't have to limit yourself to freezing to preserve the largesse.

Dried fruits are delicious too. Last year there were more pears on our tree than we could possibly eat, stew up or give away. Remembering how good the dried pears were that we once bought at a roadside fruit stand, we decided to try drying some of our own. We simply washed the pears and sliced them vertically, about four slices apiece, seeds, stem and all. Then we took off two of our window screens and hosed them off thoroughly. We laid one down and spread the sliced pears on it and then covered it with the other screen. The wooden frames touched each other and sealed out insects. To further ensure that the pears wouldn't be attacked, we placed the whole thing on top of the sloping roof of our house. Flies, we had learned, do not venture much higher than twenty feet from the ground. After two or three days, we turned all the pear slices over and put them up for another couple of days. When we brought them down, they were perfect—the moisture had been dried out yet they were still soft enough

Homemade drying rack

to eat. We then packed them into large jars, stirring them occasionally and finally sealing them tightly. Now, a year later, we are still enjoying the dried pears as an after-dinner treat. This is a perfect example of how to extend the bounties of summer through the less bountiful winter and spring periods. Incidentally, we did the same thing with a lug of apricots we bought for a dollar from a nearby farm; and our daughter had great success with a donated box of peaches.

Smoking

There's nothing quite like a chunk of well-smoked fish for flavor and economy (the latter applies especially if you have smoked it yourself). Many people believe that smoking fish (and other vittles) is a difficult process. Nothing could be further from the truth. All it takes to smoke fish or meat is a source of smoke and some kind of container to retain the smoke.

One of the simplest arrangements consists of a small electric hotplate, available at any hardware store, and an enclosure made from wire and aluminum foil. If you already have the hotplate, you can build this entire rig for less than 50 cents and a few minutes of your

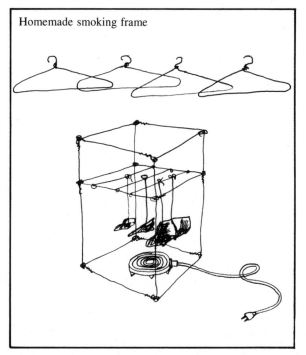

Homemade smoking frame

time. First, get a length of heavy wire 25 feet long. The type used for coat hangers is easy to bend yet substantial enough for the framework. (You can use coat hangers if you wish. Just clip off the hook, straighten them out, and twist the ends together. Each one gives about 34 inches of wire.) Bend the wire into a simple, rectangular box about two feet long and one foot square. Add some cross pieces from which to hang the food to be smoked; two or three will be plenty. Doubling the wire on these will prevent sagging under a heavy load. Cover the entire framework with aluminum foil and crimp the foil around the wire.

Next, obtain some hickory or other hard wood chips or sawdust and place them directly on the plugged-in hot plate. Cut up your fish or other food, pierce with plain wire and hang from the crosspieces inside your smoker. Carefully place the loaded smoker over the hot plate. Within a short time, the smoker will be full of warm, fragrant smoke.

You can regulate the amount of smoke and heat by turning the hot plate down or off periodically. A little practice will demonstrate how much smoke and heat to apply to a given quantity of fish or other food.

Ordinary fish, whole or in large chunks, will smoke thru in less than one day of very low heat and minimal smoke. After all, fish is easily cooked. Meats will take longer but then we don't really recommend anyone eating U.S. meat since it is so loaded with chemicals as to be both worthless and dangerous to one's health.

This type of smoker can be used wherever electricity is available. If you are one of those fortunates who live far from modern civilization, you can build yourself an outdoor smoker as follows: Construct a wooden shelter to any convenient size, anywhere from a small shed to one perhaps six feet square and eight or ten feet tall. The wood can be logs or poles and the siding anything convenient. You can either place crosspieces inside from which to hang the fish, meat or hams, or build horizontal framed squares of ordinary one-inch mesh chicken wire on which to toss the food to be smoked.

Next dig a shallow pit or cover an area on the floor with cobble stones. What you want to achieve is a cool smoke; thus your fire should be small and made from green hardwoods such as oak, hickory, and birch. Alder, willow, and similar woods are fine, but stay away from the soft, sappy woods such as pine and fir. From here on, it's just common sense and some experience. Place your meats and fish on the frames or hang them from the crosspieces. Build a *small*, smoky fire and then go about your business. You can expect the smoking process to do its flavorful work in twenty-four to forty-eight hours.

You can apply all kinds of fancy touches to the food before smoking. Try rubbing the pieces with spices, chili powder, honey, or garlic. If they are somewhat dry at the start, rub on some butter or a high-quality cooking oil or margarine.

By experimenting with this fascinating way to add good food at low cost to your table, you'll become a smoking expert in a short time. A family I know re-smokes all the ham they buy; this adds immeasurably to the flavor of storebought ham and sausage.

Canning and Freezing

So much has been written by experts on these subjects that I refer you to their work. To find out how you can freeze and can surplus foods of all types, write away for these free U.S.D.A. booklets. Address your order to United States Department of Agriculture, Washington, D.C. 20250.

For canning:
Home Canning of Fruits and Vegetables; Rev. 1967, 32 pages, illustrated. Catalog No. A 1.77:8/5.
Home Canning Meat and Poultry; 1966, 24 pages, illustrated. Catalog No. A 1.77:106.

For freezing:
Home Freezing of Fruits and Vegetables; Rev. 1967, 48 pages, illustrated. Catalog No. A 1.77:10/5.
Home Freezing of Meat and Fish; Rev. 1966, 24 pages, illustrated. Catalog No. A 1.77:93/3.
Home Freezing of Poultry; Rev. 1967, 24 pages, illustrated. Catalog No. A 1.77:70/3.

These booklets consist of solid, no-nonsense information that can make you an expert in the field of home food preservation. If, as often happens, the food you preserve comes to you free, your only expense will be for the materials and time involved in preserving the food. Bradford Angier, who writes about living off the land (see his *How To Live in the Woods on $10 a Week*) describes how people who live in the wilder parts of the United States and Canada are able to acquire enough meat to last all year from just one moose or elk. By preserving some through smoking and some through canning or freezing, a rural family can produce enough variety in their meat diet to make them the envy of the city folks who are shelling out two and three dollars for one pound of beef.

Dry and Liquid Storage Methods

In the October 1973 issue of *Organic Gardening and Farming*, there is a fine article on how to preserve foods in a very simple manner. Basically, it involves creating a root cellar where fruits and vegetables may be preserved in dry sand, hay, or other insulative materials. The major effort lies in building the various bins and storage boxes to be fitted into an area with a dry, low-temperature environment. A layer of sand is spread on the bottom of each container. Then a layer of the food to be preserved, say carrots, is placed on the sand. Make sure that the individual vegetables do not touch each other. Cover the vegetables with another layer of sand and make another layer. Dry grains such as wheat and corn are placed in dry containers and kept cool and rodent-free. Incidentally, you can add a picturesque touch to your storage area/root cellar by hanging some ears of corn or bunches of dried herbs from the ceiling. Onions, squash, pumpkins, and other easy-to-store items are merely placed in the dry, cool storage area. Keeping power depends on the original freshness of the food. All root crops can be preserved this way.

The Earnests, authors of the article, have originated a no-work method of liquid storage. For example, they place washed cucumbers in jars, add dry mustard, salt, and honey and fill the jars with vinegar. After shaking and sealing, the pickles make themselves in about two weeks. No heat, no cooking, no trouble.

Other vegetables can be preserved in water-vinegar solutions or in dill brine made by diluting one cup of white vinegar with two cups of water and adding one or more sprigs of dill to suit your taste. Tomatoes, cabbage, cauliflower, and peppers keep well in this no-cooking, liquid preservative. As the Earnests say, "There's something very comforting about being surrounded by a winter's food—stepping around full bins in the cellar and ducking under swaying bunches in the attic, touching aromatic herbs whose fragrance at times fills the house. We all benefit. The whole family works together to bring in the harvest, which we enjoy at leisure during the cold months. I probably benefit most of all, spending less time bending over a hot stove cooking and preserving and more time outside watching the garden grow." That holds true no matter how you preserve your foods.

Preserving Eggs

You can buy sodium silicate, otherwise known as waterglass, at a drug supply house or hardware store. Place eggs in a jar and cover with this liquid. They'll keep for months simply because the sodium silicate shuts out all air. Or coat the eggs with wax, the heavier the coat the better. People packing stores for long boat voyages use this method and report good keeping qualities.

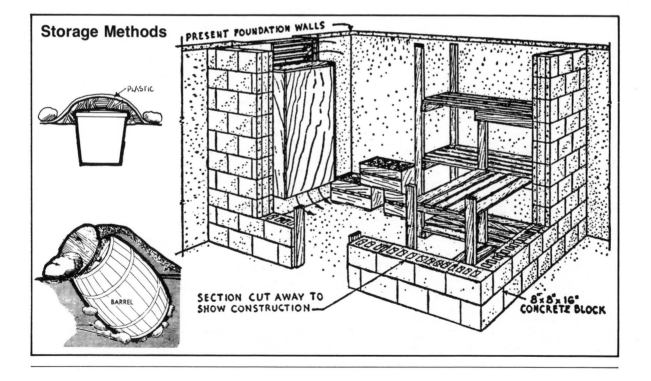

Storage Methods

PRESENT FOUNDATION WALLS

PLASTIC

BARREL

SECTION CUT AWAY TO SHOW CONSTRUCTION

8"x 8"x 16" CONCRETE BLOCK

Robert Altman

In case you have to use a supermarket

What You'll Learn:
That most of the 8,000-odd items in
a supermarket are not worth buying.
What to avoid and why.

Did you ever admire the rows of beautiful rainbow-colored containers stacked neatly at the supermarket? Don't be naive enough to think the companies threw these colorful containers in for free. When you buy a fancy package, here's what you're paying for:

- The creative design
- Preliminary and final art work
- The very expensive color printing plates
- Printing press time and material
- The filling of the package by electrical machinery
- Further packaging in a shipping carton
- The labor to put the package out on the shelf
- The labor to check it out and put it in your take-home bag

That's a lot of bills for you to pay, and you should know that some packages cost as much as 10 cents on a 50- to 60-cent item. When you shop, buy food; don't waste your money on inedible packages that clutter up your trash can and add to the waste pollution problem.

And while we're on the subject, when you shop for food, keep away from other sorts of products. Don't load your basket with cooking utensils, motor oil, clothing, and all the rest of the overpriced junk that the market would like you to buy. You can always buy these things for less in the proper store. Don't pay a hundred percent more for something just because it's convenient. As a matter of fact, when you need some item for the kitchen or the home, check your local flea market, rummage sale, Salvation Army, or Goodwill store first. You'd be amazed at how little you can pay for things at these outlets.

Skip Chewing Gum, Sugared or Sugarless

Of all the time-wasting, jaw-tiring, idiotic habits forced on people by advertising, the chewing of gum has to take one of the top trophies. Here's the problem: The sugared variety rots teeth. The non-sugared variety is expensive and creates a flow of digestive juices that trickles into the stomach for no useful purpose. Do you have to chew on something? Maybe you ought to gnaw on the end of a toothpick if you're that nervous.

Soft Drinks

The average American drinks about twenty gallons of soft drinks a year. The result is that soft-drink manufacturers get very rich and everyone else gets rotten teeth, among other things. You don't hear more about how destructive soft drinks are because the manufacturers spend millions of dollars on advertising to tell you how wonderful their products are. The people who control the media don't dare bite the hand that feeds them, and no one else can outspend the big spenders in opposition advertising. Sugar *in any form* is poison (see Chapter 9), and every twelve-ounce bottle of soft drink has about *six teaspoons* of sugar in it. Just ask an honest doctor or dentist to tell you the truth about soft drinks. For example, Dr. D. A. Collins writes in *Your Teeth, A Handbook of Dental Care for the Whole Family*, "Families that allow concentrated refined sugars, particularly in the form of cookies, cakes, candies and sweetened beverages, make the child dependent on sweets. With the development of his sweet tooth will come a high incidence of cavities. The results will be pain, loss of teeth, high dental bills and deformed mouths."

If that doesn't convince you, take a look at some more dramatic evidence:

At the Naval Medical Research Institute we put human teeth in cola beverage and found that they softened and started to dissolve within a short period. They became soft within two days.

In the intervening years 1943-1950 we have made numerous studies of the effect of these cola beverages upon the teeth of rats, dogs and monkeys. One of our technicians became so expert in judging the conditions of the surface of the molar teeth of rats that she could tell those that had had one drink of cola beverage amounting to 2½ teaspoons or 10 milliliters. We have published data indicating that the molar teeth of rats are dissolved down to the gum line, if the rats are well fed but given nothing to drink except cola beverage for a period of six months.*

Data have been published indicating that the cola beverages contain substantial amounts of caffeine. These cola beverages deserve careful consideration not only in relation to our national problem of poor teeth but in relation to our numerous cases of gastric ulcers, and welfare of our children.

The acidity of cola beverages, which the biochemist expresses as pH, is 2.6 or about the same as vinegar. The sugar content masks the acidity and children little realize they are drinking this strange mixture of phosphoric acid, sugar, caffeine, coloring and flavoring matter.**

Although a healthy liver is vital to well-being and is perhaps a main defense against cancer, the incidence of liver damage in the United States, including often fatal cirrhosis, is said to be increasing rapidly even among children. This problem once confined to chronic alcoholics is now common among social drinkers, overweight individuals, people harmed by drugs or chemicals, and those whose diets are inadequate.

Some physicians consider that the appalling consumption of soft drinks—60 million bottles daily of one brand alone—is a major cause.†

It's just not worth it to give in to your children when they beg for the junk Madison Avenue is hawking.

Instead of buying soft drinks, make your own from healthful ingredients. Serve fresh orange juice, apple juice, and milk drinks with non-sugar flavorings. Or try a punch with lots of ice, lemon juice, grapefruit or pineapple juice.

Candy, Cakes, and Cookies

Sugar is a non-food and has no place on your dining table, so you can scratch these items permanently (again, refer to Chapter 9). Not only will you save shopping money, but you'll save money on doctor and dentist bills at the same time. In addition, you'll enjoy better health, more energy, and longer life. Here are some alternatives to sugar-filled junk foods:

- honey (but go easy)
- fresh fruits
- sesame seeds
- peanut butter
- cashew butter
- nuts of all kinds
- coconut
- citron
- prunes
- dates
- carob confections
- melons

Snacks

One of the easiest ways to exceed your budget while strolling down the aisles of a market is to pick up those tempting packages of snack goods. Just imagining the taste of potato chips, the satisfying crunch of corn chips, or the filling, salty chompiness of pretzels is enough to make some people reach for one or more of these snack foods automatically. On top of that, children who have been introduced to these fun-to-eat tidbits keep clamoring for more—aided and abetted, of course, by an endless stream of commercials on TV.

There are several good reasons for avoiding this pitfall. One has to do with the high cost of the snack items relative to the amount of food actually in the package. Regarding potato chips, for instance, divide the weight of the contents into the price of the package, and you discover that you are being charged over a dollar per pound for food that costs less than ten cents per pound in the vegetable department. The second and equally important reason for avoiding snack foods is that most of them are fried in deep fat. The combination of starch with hot fat is one of the most indigestible and harmful mixtures you can eat, as almost any doctor will tell you. Do your family the favor of resisting these foods. You'll find ideas for healthful substitutes throughout this book.

Coffee and Tea

With beverage prices rising out of sight along with everything else, and caffeine under study for its effects on the human heart, it's time to start thinking in terms of healthy do-it-yourself beverages. Almost any grain such as wheat, barley, or rye can be coarsely ground, roasted in the oven and used to make a palatable boiled or percolated beverage. These substitutes were commonly employed in wartime by various nations whose supply of coffee was limited.

Tea is even easier. For example, there's wild mint growing just about everywhere in the United States.

* *Journal Nutrition*, 1949. Vol. 39, 313.
** "The Prevention Method for Better Health," J. I. Rodale and staff.
† *Lets Get Well*, Adelle Davis; Harcourt Brace Javanovich, Inc.

Gather some, dry it, and use the leaves just as you would ordinary tea leaves. You may want to try some of the more exotic teas such as comfrey, sassafras, alfalfa, and birch. All are tasty; most are better for you than the imported leaf.

While we're on the subject of drink, it's important that you make certain that your drinking water is pure. If it isn't, buy distilled drinking water, distill tap water yourself (there are small distillers now on sale), or obtain your water from a spring known to be pure. There's no point in eating healthy foods if the water you drink isn't first rate.

Alcoholic Beverages

One of the fastest ways to run your food bill up is to buy a lot of alcoholic beverages. While I'm not on the stump on behalf of the teetotalers of the world, I *am* on the stump to keep your food bills down.

Alcoholic beverages—beer, wine, whiskey, vodka, brandy, rum, etc.—are not foods by any stretch of the imagination. Therefore, if you are really concerned about your ever-mounting food bills, buy a hundred pounds of whole wheat instead of a bottle of medium-priced bourbon. The wheat will last you much longer, give you much greater returns health-wise, and will come in a lot handier a lot more often. And you can't get a hangover from home-baked bread.

But if you just can't do without a little nip now and then, a couple of recipes for homemade wine follow. These are old farmstyle methods that work as well today as they did when they were recorded in the mid-1800s.

A legal point first: You can make up to 200 gallons of wine a year for home use if you obtain a license from the Alcohol Tax Unit of the Internal Revenue Service. If you want to go into distilled liquors, then you've got to talk at length with these same people.

BLACKBERRY WINE

Gather the berries when ripe on a dry day, measure and bruise them. To every gallon of berries add 1 quart of boiling water. Let the mixture stand 24 hours, stirring occasionally. Strain off the liquor into a cask, and to every gallon add one pound of honey. Cork tight and let it stand until October and you will have wine for use without any further steaming or boiling.

GRAPE WINE

Heat the grapes slightly in a large kettle with very little water and then crush through a strainer until you have one quart of juice. To this add 3 quarts of water and 2½ pounds of honey. Keep in an open barrel for 19 days, covering with muslin to protect from insects. Then put in a closed cask, fasten and bung, and set aside until spring. Then rack off and bottle.

These recipes are simple to follow if you have the correct ingredients and equipment. To make your finished product especially appealing, make up some labels on parchment paper. They can be printed from a wood block or simply written by hand with an old goosequill.

Chain Restaurants

Chain restaurants are cousins to supermarkets. If you ever sit in on a board meeting for a large restaurant chain, you won't believe your ears. The customer has absolutely no status at all. He only exists as a body to fill up a seat, a stomach to be filled with the cheapest food dispensed at the highest prices. Most of these places seek to delude you into thinking you've been well fed at the end of a meal. They cater, of course, to the person who thinks that a fried piece of meat on a plastic sponge bun is a meal in itself. Almost everything served in a typical chain is fried, and the soup is a concoction of chemicals warmed in plain tap water. Ugh, I could go on for pages. But your own sense of taste will convince you. Do yourself a favor. Carry something good to eat wherever you go and leave the chain restaurants to languish in their fried-fat fumes.

Grape vine

Blackberry

Dandelion

Elderberry

What you should know about sugar

What You'll Learn:
That sugar is a slow (sometimes
not so slow) poison.

Author's note: We are grateful to Mick and Lini of the LA *Free Press* for this definitive and forceful review of a product that comprises as much as *half* of some American diets.

This week, in answer to many requests we've had from our readers, we'd like to talk about sugar and what its effects are on the human body. Of all the foods we eat, sugar is one of the most harmful and there are myriad reasons for avoiding it.

—The sugar we usually eat is not a whole food but rather the extract of a tropical plant. When we eat sugar our body's automatic response is to swallow it without chewing it.

—Sugar is extremely alkaline. When we swallow it the stomach is paralyzed for one to three minutes by the shock it produces on our system. In reaction to this strong alkaline substance, the stomach secretes a tremendous amount of acid in an attempt to neutralize it.

—When the sugar leaves the stomach it takes this excess acid with it and enters the duodenum, still in an undigested form. Because of this excess acid, the duodenum lets it pass through again without neutralizing it and consequently it goes on to pollute the rest of the body.

—In order to digest sugar the intestines have to draw on the mineral reserves in the body and this produces tooth decay, falling hair and weak bone structure. (It might be interesting for you to know that the condition of the teeth is a good indication of the condition of the entire skeleton.) In addition, since a great deal of oxygen is consumed during this process, there is a shortage of oxygen in the brain and consequently the mental capacity is reduced.

—When the sugar reaches the blood stream even more problems arise. Our pancreas is designed to deal only with natural sugars. When it encounters a substance as powerful as refined sugar one of two things can happen. Since it is the function of the pancreas to neutralize sugar, there is a panic reaction and a great deal of insulin is secreted. If the pancreas is weak and this condition continues diabetes may develop. In most cases, however, the pancreas is strong enough to remain operative and it secretes *too much* insulin. This neutralizes most of the sugar in the blood. The result is hypo-glycemia—low blood sugar, a condition which nine out

of 10 Americans suffer from to some degree.

—Hypoglycemia manifests itself in countless ways. Some of the symptoms are tiredness, irritability, sudden fits of anger, irrationality, poor memory and hostility. If you have ever suddenly found yourself exhausted for no apparent reason and desiring sweets then there is a good chance that you are suffering from low blood sugar.

—The problem becomes more complicated because when you have hypoglycemia you are drawn to even more sugar. If you eat more sugar you will feel better for a while, but soon you will start to feel tired and listless again. The only way of remedying this is by eating more sugar. In this manner, sugar produces an addiction that is just as real and powerful as that of any drug.

—When hypoglycemia develops our mentality suffers greatly. We become prone to fear, anxiety, worry, hatred, sudden fits of violence. It becomes easy for us to lie since our judgement is so clouded that it is difficult for us to see that in many cases it would be easier for us to tell the truth.

—Mothers who indulge their children's sweet tooth with sugar are often repaid with temper tantrums and unruly behavior. The child who screams and cries constantly is almost invariably a lover of sweets. If the wise parent removes all sweets from the child's diet there will be an almost miraculous improvement in the child's behavior within a very short time.

—Much of the food available in the so-called health food stores contain brown sugar or yellowed sugar. There is a general superstition among health-minded people that these sugars are in some way superior to refined white sugar. In reality, however, brown sugar is simply refined sugar with the molasses added again to give it color. Sugar is sugar, regardless of what it is called or what color it is, and should be avoided at all times.

—Since sugar is so powerfully alkaline, it will burn the tongue of a baby. Only after repeated use do our tastes become so jaded that we enjoy it. If you refrain from eating sugar for several months and then try eating it, you too will find the taste unpleasant and the reaction it produces both immediate and powerful. If you cease using sugar your taste will gradually return to natural proportions, and if you chew your food very thoroughly you will be surprised at the sweetness you will discover in such simple foods as carrots, squash, onions and grains.

—Many of you may be asking the question "What about honey or molasses?" These are merely another form of sugar and should also be avoided for the same reasons. Although honey is a natural substance, it has almost the same effect upon the human body as sugar. Molasses is nothing more than the pulp that remains after sugar has been refined. Although this may be disheartening you owe it to yourself to let your body have a chance to develop its natural tastes again. Honey causes your taste to become jaded in the same manner as sugar does. If you stop eating it for a while, you will not only be giving your body a much needed rest, but you will have the opportunity to taste the real SWEETNESS of foods that you would have missed otherwise. If, after not eating honey for some time, you find yourself drawn to it again, by all means have some. The taste will be less stimulating than you imagined it would be and you will find that you are listless and grouchy the following day.

—The only way to cure hypoglycemia is to stop eating sugar and other sweets. Although you may have a reaction it will soon pass and your energy will return. Foods that greatly assist the body in overcoming hypoglycemia are brown rice, aduki beans and squash.

Now, that's a powerful indictment of a product that is consumed in large quantities in America. The average person is believed to consume about a third of a pound of sugar per *day*. What do others say about this non-food item (non-food in the sense that it contributes nothing but calories)?

"Sugar is a nutritionally bankrupt substance...," says Frances Dahl, Nutritionist with the Marin County Department of Health. And Dr. John Yudkin, a University of London nutritionist and author of *Sweet and Dangerous* suggests that sugar is involved in coronary artery disease and adds that evidence against sugar is even more conclusive than it is against cholesterol.

Harvard professor of nutrition, Dr. Jean Mayer reports that 100 pounds of sugar is equal to 57 pounds of body fat (just about what many people have in excess weight).

One of the major problems with sugar is that it is present in almost all prepared foods. And even though the cost of sugar is rising it is still found in such seemingly innocent foods as bouillon cubes and non-dairy creamer. Further, sugar is the major ingredient in many items such as cola drinks, cake, and donuts.

One of the great pioneers in nutritional research,

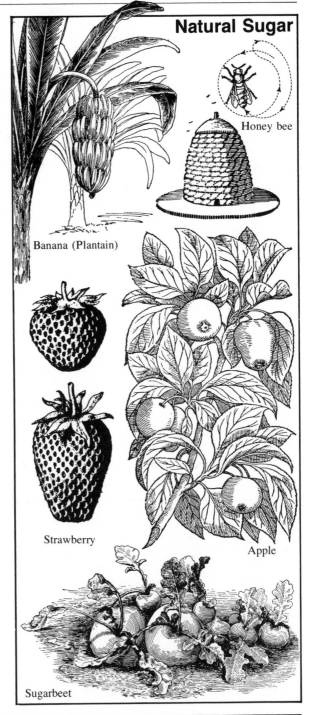

Natural Sugar

Banana (Plantain)

Honey bee

Strawberry

Apple

Sugarbeet

J. I. Rodale, contributed an immense store of basic information concerning sugar and its effect on the human body. In one of his classic volumes, *The Complete Book of Food and Nutrition*, the many condemning references to sugar ought to convince any intelligent reader to exclude this non-food from his or her diet. Here is an example (but we recommend that you read it for yourself in the nearest library or book store):

Concentrated pure sugar is a drug, unrelated to anything that occurs naturally. It throws off the calcium-phosphorus balance and disrupts this important phase of your body machinery. Because it has been robbed of its B vitamins, it latches on to these wherever it finds them—namely in your digestive tract. Thus, the person who eats sugar is bound to be short on B vitamins. Result? Nervousness, skin troubles, digestive problems and a host of other disorders which lead to much more serious trouble later on.

Rodale points out that sugar substitutes—molasses, maple syrup, and honey—are also fraught with hazards and he advises readers not to consume too much of them.

Rodale's book goes on to quote a speech given by M. H. Walsh, instructor in clinical nutrition at the University of California. In it, Walsh replies to the contention that sugar is a food by saying that if it were, it would be fed to animals by hog, beef and poultry producers. The fact that sugar is not fed to these animals is solid proof that sugar is not really a food but rather a profit-making condiment/flavoring.

In reviewing Rodale's material further we find that sugar is responsible for dental caries (cavities), low blood sugar (eating sugar brings up the level momentarily but it plunges down as natural insulin is circulated), asthmas, alcoholism, neuroses, fatigue, rheumatic fever, ulcers, depression and on through a medical chamber of horrors.

From the author's own experience comes this true tale. A nephew had a kneecap removed surgically because it no longer functioned as a kneecap. In tracing back the problem it was discovered that the young boy had been drinking a six-pack of a common cola each and every day for years. Apparently, the phosphoric acid in the Coke leached out all the calcium in the boy's system including that *behind* the kneecap. Had he continued to drink the sugar-loaded soft drink, he would have ended up with no skeleton.

Conclusion

There's lots of evidence around that sugar is the worst nutritional enemy of many people. So why not try this test. Eliminate all or nearly all sugar from your diet for six weeks or so. See if you don't feel peppier, less tired at the end of the day, have better digestion and, not incidentally, save lots of money. With sugar at an all-time high price, it's an expensive means to bad health. By no sugar we mean no bakery products, candy, ice cream, soft drinks, chewing gum, canned fruit, and so forth. Satisfy your conditioned sugar hunger with fresh fruit, raisins, dates and such.

Date palm

PART II
HOW TO COOK
ON A DOLLAR
A DAY

The Golden Rule:
eat less,
waste nothing

What You'll Learn:
How to develop an attitude about
how much food you really need, and
how to use what you don't eat.

The first man to warn against over-eating lived in medieval Europe. Luigi Cornaro, a 16th century Venetian, came from a wealthy family and wasted his early years in such riotous living, drunkenness and gluttony that by the time he was forty, degenerative diseases threatened to kill him. Given no hope by his physicians, Cornaro retired to a small country estate and took stock of himself. He was an intelligent man; well-educated for his times, and capable of solid reasoning. He came to the conclusion that the human body was designed to function most efficiently and well on the minimum amount of food it takes to maintain normal weight and strength. Over-eating was not simply a waste of food but a definite strain and burden on the body organs. He decided to experiment on himself and found that an intake of about fourteen ounces of solid food daily, with a pint of wine best satisfied his particular needs. He ate only the plainest and simplest foods: coarse whole grain bread, a little meat—usually fowl—and a green salad. Calorie values were unknown five hundred years ago, so Cornaro concerned himself only with quantity.

He found that in his own case the balance between enough and too much was so delicate, due to his damaged organs, that the addition of only two ounces more than he required would produce a severe digestive disturbance. This was perhaps fortunate, for it strengthened his already formidable resolve, and he was able to stick to his diet so faithfully that he regained his health. He became a noted architect and one of the leading citizens of the powerful Venetian republic, fathered a large family, and lived comfortably to the ripe old age of 102.

Cornaro wrote of his experiences and advised others to follow his example, but he prescribed no diets, and suggested that each person should experiment with the needs of his own body to discover the kinds of food and the minimum amount of food necessary to maintain health, weight, and vigor. He recognized that this would vary with the individual and the kind of exercise and work performed. But, although Cornaro's work has been widely read, translated into many languages, and published many times over, people rarely show the resolution and will-power to follow his advice. One notable exception was John D. Rockefeller, Sr., who recovered his health and lived to the age of 96 through careful attention to a minimum diet. In his case, as in Cornaro's, it must be pointed out that severe digestive troubles made Rockefeller's attention to diet imperative. For most of us, food and the pleasures of eating are so important that we can seldom summon the will-power to practice such Spartan restraint. But the closer we come to ingesting minimal individual requirements, the greater will be our reward in improved health and comfortable long life.

If you have ever gone into your kitchen looking for something to eat and found nothing appealing, you probably felt disappointed. But this momentary disappointment is a small price to pay for a slender and healthy body. And if you do manage to keep your kitchen completely free of snacks and excess food items except for fresh fruit, vegetables, seeds and nuts, the temptation to constantly nibble on something will slowly go away.

I recall a friend who was extremely fond of little cans of deviled ham. He would purchase them in quantity and eat them whenever he felt a bit hungry, frustrated, or simply bored. His weight began creeping up because with these prepared meats he usually had crackers and a glass of milk. The 300 or 400 calories that he added to his daily diet this way was all that was required to produce a steady and inexorable weight gain. One day, in discussing this with him casually, I suggested that the simplest way to break this habit was just not to buy the little cans of ham in the first place. He took the advice and not only did he save money, his weight returned to normal. A common sense approach? You bet it is, but one that unfortunately many millions of Americans do not practice.

Another friend of ours, who had moved away several years ago, kept lamenting in her letters about the way she was gaining weight. Recently we spent a week visiting in her home and found out why. Each evening before dinner it was her custom to serve drinks. This in itself was not the culprit, since she never had more than one martini. But the cocktail hour was an excuse for her to drag out all manner of tasty little appetizers and snacks—cheeses, olives, smoked oysters, sardines, dips, chips and crackers. While we sat there chatting, our friend continually helped herself to these high caloric appetizers. Since she ate only a modest dinner after this (small wonder!) she couldn't understand why those pounds kept adding up. After I added up the calories contained in her nibbling, she saw the light. Not only was she consuming *more* calories during the cocktail hour than she did for dinner, but the money it

took to buy these extravagant little goodies often surpassed the outlay for the entire dinner.

You'll find these suggestions repeated throughout this book, but here again are the basic rules for cutting down on food intake:

- Buy only natural foods in their natural state.
- Buy no convenience or snack foods whatsoever.
- Prepare a shopping list if you do have to shop at a conventional market. This is most important, since the Madison Avenue boys sit up nights developing ways to coax you into buying snack foods on impulse. So take your shopping list, wear a pair of blinders, and march through the traps with the resolute purpose of buying only the items on your list, the foods you need to stay healthy and retain your normal weight.
- Go easy on even the good stuff. Follow the example of our old friend, Luigi, the Slender Italian Renaissance Man.
- Remember that human beings need a good balance of five elements: carbohydrates, fats, protein, vitamins, and minerals. A well-balanced meal will provide these necessities in their proper proportions. To

Robert Altman

How To Use Your Leftovers

Egg yolks:
   baked custard
   cakes, cookies
   homemade noodles
   mock hollandaise
      sauce
   scrambled eggs

Egg whites:
   cakes
   meringue
   soufflés

Sour Cream:
   beef stroganoff
   cakes, cookies
   salad dressings
   sauce for vegetables

Cooked meats, poultry, and fish:
   casseroles
   creamed foods
   curries
   hash
   patties
   potpies
   salads
   sandwiches

Cooked snap beans, lima beans, corn, peas, carrots:
   casseroles
   creamed dishes
   meat, poultry, or
      fish pies
   salads
   sauces
   scalloped vegetables
   soups
   stews
   vegetables in cheese
      sauce

Cooked leafy vegetables, chopped:
   creamed or scalloped
      vegetables
   omelets
   soufflés
   soups

Vegetable cooking liquids:
   gravies
   sauces
   soups
   stews

Cooked rice, noodles, macaroni, spaghetti:
   baked macaroni and
      cheese
   casseroles
   macaroni salad
   meat or cheese loaf
   spanish rice

Hard-cooked egg or yolk:
   casseroles
   egg sauce
   garnish
   salads
   sandwiches
   thousand island
      dressing

Buttermilk:
   cakes, cookies
   quick breads

Meat or poultry drippings and broth:
   gravies
   sauces
   soups
   stews

Cooked potatoes:
   fried or creamed
      potatoes
   meat or potato patties
   meat-pie topping
   potatoes in cheese sauce
   salads
   soups, stews, or
      chowders

Cooked or canned fruits:
   fruit cups
   fruit sauces
   gelatin desserts
   prune cake
   quick breads
   salads
   shortcake
   upside-down cake
   yeast breads

Fruit cooking liquids or fruit syrups:
   fruit cups
   fruit sauces
   fruit drinks
   gelatin mixtures
   tapioca puddings

Cooked wheat, oat, or corn cereals:
   fried cereal
   meat loaf or patties
   soufflés
   puddings

Bread:
   bread pudding
   croutons
   dry crumbs for
      breading meat,
      poultry, or fish
   fondues
   french toast
   meat loaf, salmon
      loaf
   sardine puff
   stuffings

tip the balance with in-between-meal snacks is unnecessary and wasteful.

Waste Nothing

Consider this: If you lose twenty percent of the food value of the things you buy in just plain physical waste, another twenty percent due to improper cooking (heating destroys vitamins), and still another twenty percent in failure to digest properly, it's possible that more than half of what you buy goes down the assorted drains. Corrective measures are in order: (1) Don't waste a speck; (2) cook foods as little as possible to preserve their nutritional values; and (3) eat correctly and exercise to make sure your body is able to extract the full nutritional value from the foods you eat.

You'll be tempted to eat up the balance of a dish if you have prepared too much. This is the road to obesity and wastefulness. Cook adequate servings, just enough for one meal, particularly for foods that are unpalatable when reheated. But if you *do* have leftovers, use them as shown in the chart opposite.

The French have a centuries-old method for using everything up. It's called the "pot au feu," and is a kettle of soup that simmers on the back of most country people's stoves all the time. This ever-new dish contains bits of everything that might have gone to waste. Naturally, it changes its character and flavor as days go by and that's good. Try this in your quest for good eating for less money.

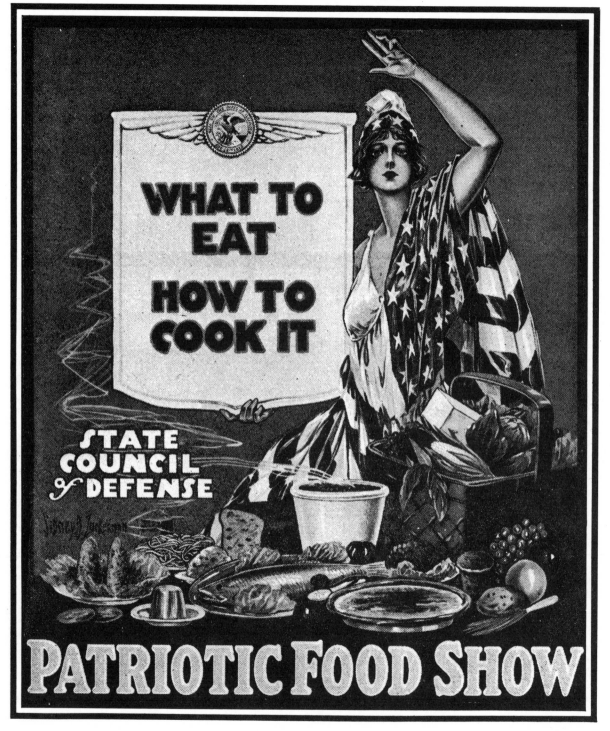

Sample menus on a dollar a day

What You'll Learn:
How to prepare menus for under a
dollar a day. These menus are
designed for two but can be expanded
to feed any number.

A Typical Well-Balanced Menu

Breakfast:
 Honey-Almond Brown Rice Delight
 Milk
 Sliced Fresh Oranges
Lunch:
 Savory Onion Soup
 Homebaked Bread
 Butter
 Dates
Dinner:
 Enchiladas Baja
 Sprout, cabbage and green pepper salad
 Watermelon wedges

HONEY-ALMOND BROWN RICE DELIGHT

4 tablespoons brown rice
1 tablespoon shelled almonds
1 tablespoon honey
2 cups skim milk (reconstituted)
 Simmer rice until tender. Add chopped almonds and honey. Serve with milk, warmed if desired.

SAVORY ONION SOUP

¼ tablespoons drippings
⅛ cup chopped onions
1 bouillon cube dissolved in one cup soup stock
¼ cups water or one if stock is used
 Sauté onions in drippings. Dissolve cube in hot soup stock.

Cost Analysis, Well Balanced Menu

	Cost in cents	Cooked weight (oz.)		Cost in cents	Cooked weight (oz.)
Breakfast:			**Dinner:**		
Brown rice	.04	6	Soy analog	.13	4
Almonds	.10	1	Tortillas	.08	4
Honey	.06	1	Onion	.03	4
Skim milk	.15	16	Tomato sauce	.05	4
Two whole oranges	.20	12	Chili powder	.02	—
Totals	.55	36	Garlic clove	.01	—
			Olives	.08	2
Lunch:			Cheese	.16	2
Onions	.10	16	Sprouts (homegrown		
Bouillon cube	.08	—	from 1 oz. seed)	.05	3
Sourdough bread	.20	16	Cabbage	.04	4
Butter	.10	12	Green pepper	.03	1
Soup stock		16	Oil and vinegar	.05	3
Dates (8)	.16	12	Watermelon wedges	.04	8
Totals	.64	72	Totals	.77	39
			Grand totals	**$1.96**	**147**

Add onions and remaining water and cook to desired taste and consistency. Season with homegrown herbs such as basil, thyme or oregano, salt, pepper. Serve hot.

ENCHILADAS BAJA

1 tablespoon bacon drippings or other fat
½ cup soy analog
½ cup chopped onion
1 clove garlic minced
4 tortillas
½ cup tomato sauce
1 tablespoon chili powder
4 tablespoons grated cheese
4 olives
salt, pepper
    Sauté chopped onion and garlic in fat. Presoak soy analog to hydrate. When softened, add to onions and garlic and simmer 5 minutes. In separate pan, simmer tomato sauce with chili powder and seasonings for 5 minutes. Heat additional fat or lard in frying pan and dip tortillas in for a few seconds on each side. Then dip in tomato sauce and lay on dish. Fill with one-fourth of soy mixture, add 1 tablespoon grated cheese and roll up. Pour remaining sauce on top and garnish with olives. Bake at 350° for 20 minutes.

SPROUT, CABBAGE AND GREEN PEPPER SALAD

4 tablespoons mung bean sprouts
4 tablespoons finely shredded cabbage
1 tablespoon minced green pepper
2 tablespoons oil, 1 tablespoon vinegar
salt, pepper
    Toss mixed greens with oil, vinegar and seasonings.

HOMEBAKED SOURDOUGH BREAD

4 cups freshly ground whole wheat flour
pinch salt
water to mix
    Mix 4 tablespoons flour with a little warm water. Let stand in saucer at room temperature for five days, stirring each day. When fermented, add to remaining flour in bowl and add sufficient water to make a stiff batter. Turn out on floured board and knead thoroughly. Then let the dough rise in a warm place until double in size. Punch down, knead again and let rise a second time. Turn into greased baking pan, let rise and bake at 350° for one hour.

    Most nutritionists would deem this a well-balanced diet, since the emphasis is on fresh fruits, vegetables and grains. Price per person for all three meals is 98 cents.

    The portions derived from these recipes are more than adequate. The total weight of all three meals is three and a half pounds per person. It is obvious that there will be extra food for a child or guest or something left over for the next day.

Suggested Menu for Two Featuring a Big Breakfast

Breakfast:
    Western pancakes
    Honey/Butter/Walnuts Syrup
    Roasted grain coffee or mint tea
Lunch:
    Potatoes and Ham with Cheese Sauce (Recipe page 113)
    Sliced cucumbers, splash of wild apple vinegar
    Fresh pears
Dinner:
    Tossed Salad with Potato Mayonnaise
    Banana Spice Bars (See recipe page 136)
    Alfalfa Tea

WESTERN PANCAKES

    To ½ pound freshly ground whole wheat flour, add two large eggs, ¼ cup of spray process dry milk, ¼ cup fresh ground corn meal, ¼ cup safflower or soy oil, pinch salt and water to mix into a cream-like batter. Pour on hot greased griddle to make 3 to 4 inch diameter cakes. Turn when bubbles form. Serve piping hot with syrup made from melted butter, honey and chopped walnuts. Terrific!

WILD APPLE VINEGAR

    Gather wild apples, core and crush. Strain juice into bottles and allow to ferment naturally. Presto! Free, pure, organic vinegar for your salads.

TOSSED SALAD

    To domestic greens such as lettuce and romaine, add poke, dandelion and other wild salad materials that cost no more than the time to gather them.

POTATO MAYONNAISE

½ cup baked mashed potato
1 teaspoon dry mustard
dash salt if desired
2 tablespoons wild apple vinegar

¾ cup cold pressed oil

Add mustard, salt and 1 tablespoon vinegar to mashed potato and rub through fine sieve. Beat briskly while adding remaining vinegar and oil.

ALFALFA TEA

Another freebee. Gather wild alfalfa, dry and crumble. Use like regular tea leaves. Delicious and healthful. A bit of mint will perk it up if you wish.

This menu begins with a substantial breakfast, continues with a good solid lunch and then tapers off with a light dinner. Many people sleep better if they go easy on the chow late at night. Try it yourself and see what happens.

Vegetarian Menu (one)

Breakfast:

Homemade yogurt with sunflower seeds, raisins, and walnuts

Whole wheat toast with butter and honey

Anise tea

Lunch:

Minestrone

Crackers and cheese

Fruit of the season

Dinner:

Eggplant Parmesan

Refried Beans

Dates

Homemade roasted-grain coffee

HOMEMADE YOGURT

(Recipe on page 56)

Add seeds and other items to taste.

ANISE TEA

Seeds of anise plant may be gathered wild. Steep like tea. Delicious.

MINESTRONE

1 cup thinly sliced vegetables
 (tomatoes, celery, carrots, onions)
1 tablespoon butter
1½ pints water

Cost Analysis, Big Breakfast

	Cost in cents	Cooked weight (oz.)		Cost in cents	Cooked weight (oz.)
Breakfast:			**Lunch:**		
Fresh ground wheat flour	.10	8	Potatoes with Ham and Cheese Sauce (one/half of recipe on page 113)	.40	16
Two large eggs	.16	4	Sliced cucumbers	.05	4
Powdered milk	.10	4	Wild apple vinegar	—	1
Corn meal	.02	2	Pears, two	.30	12
Oil	.10	2	*Totals*	.75	33
Butter	.10	2			
Honey	.12	2	**Dinner:**		
Walnuts	.05	1	Lettuce, romaine	.20	6
Roasted grain coffee	.01	—	Wild salad materials	—	3
Totals	.76	25	Potato mayonnaise	.18	4
			Alfalfa tea	—	16
			Totals	.38	29
			Grand totals	**1.89**	**87**

sprig parsley
bay leaf, thyme, salt/pepper
⅓ cup macaroni or spaghetti
grated Romano cheese

Sauté vegetables in butter. Add other ingredients and boil 2 minutes. Simmer until vegetables are "al dente." Serve with sprinkle of grated cheese.

EGGPLANT PARMESAN

Slice eggplant about ¼ inch thick. Dip in beaten egg to which a bit of basil, oregano or other seasoning has been added. Sauté in butter and sprinkle with Parmesan cheese. Serve hot.

REFRIED BEANS

Boil beans until tender. Mash and refry with onions and bacon fat or lard.

ROASTED GRAIN COFFEE

Toast wheat, rye or barley in pan. Grind and use like regular coffee.

Vegetarian Menu (two)

Breakfast:
   Sliced bananas
   Scotch Toast with honey
   Camomile tea
Lunch:
   Barley mushroom soup
   Raw carrot sticks
   Raspberry tea
Dinner:
   Zucchini Frittata
   Baked potato with yogurt and chives
   Spinach and sprout salad with oil, vinegar and home grown basil
   Wild clover tea

SCOTCH TOAST WITH HONEY

Beat one egg per person with 1 tablespoon milk. Spread about ½ cup rolled oats on platter. Dip whole wheat bread in egg mixture then dip both sides in the oats. Fry slowly in butter. Two slices per person with honey filling.

BARLEY MUSHROOM SOUP

Cook ¼ cup barley in 1 cup water until tender. Cook 1 grated carrot, 1 sliced onion, ⅛ lb. sliced mushrooms in oil or butter til tender. Combine with barley and 1 cup vegetable

Cost Analysis, Vegetarian One

Breakfast:	Cost in cents	Cooked weight (oz.)	Lunch:		
Yogurt made from skim milk and retained culture	.30	16	Assorted vegetables, average at 18¢/lb.	.09	8
Added seeds, raisins, nuts	.05	—	Butter	.03	.5
Whole wheat toast	.05	6	Parsley (homegrown)	—	2
Honey	.12	2	Bay leaf (gathered free)	—	—
Butter	.10	2	Thyme	.01	—
			Salt/pepper	.01	—
			Macaroni or spaghetti	.00	16
Totals	.62	30	Grated Romano	.05	.5
			Totals	.19	27
			Dinner:		
			Eggplant	.40	16
			Beans	.09	8
			Roasted grain coffee	.01	16
			Dates	.20	4
			Totals	.50	44
			Grand totals	**1.31**	**101**

Relative Diet Values

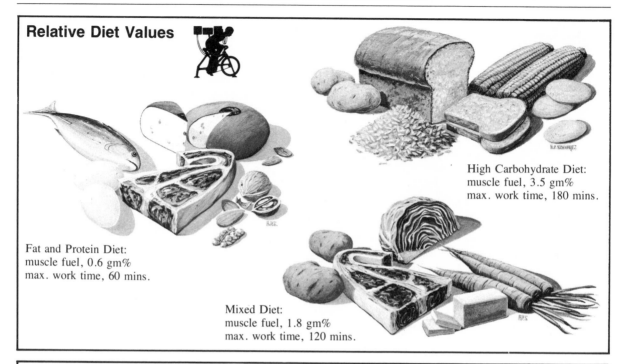

Fat and Protein Diet:
muscle fuel, 0.6 gm%
max. work time, 60 mins.

High Carbohydrate Diet:
muscle fuel, 3.5 gm%
max. work time, 180 mins.

Mixed Diet:
muscle fuel, 1.8 gm%
max. work time, 120 mins.

Cost Analysis, Vegetarian Two

Breakfast:	Cost in cents	Cooked weight (oz.)
Sliced bananas	.08	8
Scotch toast, including egg, milk and oats	.25	10
Camomile tea	.05	—
Honey	.05	1
Totals	*.43*	*19*

Lunch:		
Barley	.03	10
Carrot, two	.08	4
Onion, small	.05	4
Mushrooms	.20	4
Parsley	.05	1
Seasonings	.05	1
Raspberry tea	.06	8
Totals	*.32*	*31*

Dinner:		
Two zucchini	.18	8
Onion, small	.05	4
Clove garlic	.05	1
Potatoes, medium, two	.05	8
Yogurt	.10	4
Chives, homegrown	—	—
Spinach	.04	2
Sprouts	.05	3
Oil	.03	1
Vinegar	.02	1
Basil, homegrown	—	—
Wild clover tea	—	8
Totals	*.53*	*40*
Grand totals	**1.32**	**90**

water or stock and add sea salt to taste, finely minced home-grown parsley, and a sprinkle of paprika for color and flavor.

ZUCCHINI FRITTATA

2 medium zucchini sliced
1 small onion minced
1 clove garlic

Saute above in olive oil. Remove from pan. Beat 2 eggs with salt and pepper to taste. Fold in 2 tablespoons parmesan cheese and the cooked vegetables. Heat oil in skillet and cook mixture, turning carefully until light brown. Serve immediately if not sooner.

This is tasty vegetarian fare that will make it hard to return to expensive, heavy acid-forming meat-based meals. Note how liberal your menus can be if you don't pay those high prices for small amounts of meat and poultry. Further, this type of food is easy to digest; you don't have that fagged out feeling after lunch or dinner. Minerals and vitamins of the organic, natural kind abound in fresh-cooked or raw food such as this.

Note to superthrifty chefs: You can buy spices and herbs by the *ounce* at many natural food stores. This is much cheaper than buying them in packaged form.

Mineral-Rich Seafood Menu (one)

Breakfast:
 Scrambled eggs with herbs
 Hot biscuits and honey/butter
 Catnip tea (makes humans purr too)
Lunch:
 Homemade fry bread (See recipe page 109)
 Celery sticks
 Fruit in season
Dinner:
 Sliced tomato and watercress salad
 Squid Italienne
 Baked squash
 Chicory coffee
 Wild apples

SQUID ITALIENNE

First a word about squid. Most people feel repulsed by anything resembling an octopus which squid does. However, cleaned, sliced and simmered in a rich Italian sauce, squid competes with the most delicate scallops, shrimp, or other sea food. We ask only that you defer judgment until you make

Cost Analysis, Seafood One

Breakfast:	Cost in cents	Cooked weight (oz.)	Dinner:		
Eggs	.16	5	Tomato	.15	8
Herbs	.01	—	Watercress	.03	2
Flour	.03	12	Squid Italienne,		
Shortening	.05	3	two portions	.50	16
Tea	—	8	Squash	.10	6
			Chicory coffee	—	—
Totals	.25	28	Wild apples	—	8
			Totals	.78	40
Lunch:					
Rye bread, two slices	.06	4	Grand totals	1.69	94
Meatballs	.25	8			
Celery sticks	.10	6			
Fruit (orange, apple, pear, melon)	.25	8			
Totals	.55	26			

this recipe and try it. Further, with seafood of conventional types out of sight pricewise, squid at four pounds for a dollar (January, 1975; Monterey, California) becomes quite attractive to both purse and palate.

2 pounds squid (must be fresh)
4 tablespoons olive oil
pinch oregano
1 teaspoon chopped parsley
1 cup solid pack tomatoes or equivalent fresh
dash sherry, optional
2 cloves garlic
salt and pepper to taste

Clean squid and cut into small pieces. Wash well. Pour olive oil in pan and heat. Brown garlic, add squids, sauté about 15 minutes. Add seasonings and cook five minutes longer. Add vegetables and cover. Simmer gently about 10 minutes more or until all is tender and delicious. Serve hot over rice, spaghetti or other pasta if desired.

Mineral Rich Seafood Menu (two)

Breakfast:
    Potato pancakes
    Baked apple
    Wild sassafras tea

Lunch:
    Broiled soyburgers (see recipe page 117)
    Banana spice bars (see recipe page 136)
    Lemonade
Dinner:
    Seafood chowder
    Easy bread (see recipe page 108)
    Fresh peach cobbler (see Blackberry Slump, p. 49)
    Black tea or homemade grain coffee

POTATO PANCAKES

Grate two large potatoes. Blend with 2 tablespoons minced onion, one teaspoon minced parsley, one beaten egg, dash salt if desired. Form into round patties, fry slowly in oil, butter or lard, until browned. Serves two.

SEAFOOD CHOWDER

Cut about one pound of any low-cost fish into 2-inch pieces. Put into pot along with head and tail and add 1 cup cold water. Bring slowly to boil and cook 5 minutes. Simmer a small sliced onion in pork or bacon fat and add two sliced potatoes. Pour on one-half cup water and cook 10 minutes. Add fish in its liquor, 1 cup scalded milk, and salt and pepper. Simmer another 5 minutes and serve.

Cost Analysis, Seafood Two

	Cost in cents	Cooked weight (oz.)
Breakfast:		
Potato pancakes	.25	18
Baked apple	.20	12
Tea	—	10
Totals	.45	40
Lunch:		
Broiled soyburgers	.40	16
Banana spice bars, 2	.12	6
Lemonade	.10	8
Totals	.62	30

	Cost in cents	Cooked weight (oz.)
Dinner:		
Seafood chowder	.23	16
Easy bread	.10	6
Peach Cobbler	.20	10
Tea	.05	8
Totals	.58	40
Grand totals	**1.65**	**110**

PEACH COBBLER

(See recipe for blackberry cobbler page 49, substitute peaches.)

If you live close to a body of water, fish may be free for the catching. If so, your overall costs are that much lower. Again, it is important to discover as many sources of free and wild foods as possible. For example, close to where we are winding up this book, there are many spring salad materials in the open fields, items such as poke, wild radish, dandelion, nettles (steam the tender young leaves). We also observe lots of blackberry vines here that will produce later this summer. These could be substituted for the peaches in the cobbler.

Round-The-World Menus for Two

Breakfast:

Wild blackberry pancakes (Refer to Western pancake recipe, add black berries in abundance)
Birch syrup
Homemade grain coffee

Lunch:

English Cheese Pudding (see recipe, page 133)
Poke salad
Peach Crisp

Dinner:

Mexican Hash (see recipe, page 126)
Homemade salsa
Spearmint tea and cookies

BIRCH SYRUP

Drill holes in birches, insert hollow tube. Drain sap into buckets. Boil proceeds into thin syrup.

POKE SALAD

Gather wild poke greens, add favorite dressing, enjoy.

PEACH CRISP

Spread layer of fresh sliced peaches in bottom of pie pan. Sprinkle with mixture of oats, fresh ground whole wheat flour and butter. Dot with more butter and dribble a bit of honey on it. Bake till it bubbles and topping is brown.

HOMEMADE SALSA

Combine chopped tomatoes, onions and green chilis.

Cost Analysis, Round-The-World

	Cost in cents	Cooked weight (oz.)		Cost in cents	Cooked weight (oz.)
Breakfast:			**Dinner:**		
Wild blackberry pancakes	.28	16	Mexican hash, two portions	.58	16
Birch syrup	—	4	Tomatoes	.10	4
Homemade grain coffee	.01	8	Onions	.05	4
			Green chilis	.10	4
Totals	*.29*	*28*	Spearmint tea	—	8
Lunch:			*Totals*	*.83*	*36*
English cheese pudding, two portions	.40	12			
Poke salad	—	4	**Grand totals**	**1.97**	**.98**
Oil, vinegar	.10	2			
Peach crisp, two portions	.35	16			
Totals	*.85*	*34*			

Enjoy better bread by making your own

Dian Ooka

What You'll Learn:
How to win friends and influence
people with your homebaked bread.

Once you've baked your own bread, you won't want to go back to store-bought plastic foam ever again. The fun and joy of creating something good to eat with your own hands will more than compensate you for the time and effort expended. And there are other bonus benefits:

• Bread made from freshly ground whole wheat flour contains none of the phony chemicals and "enrichments" found in store-bought bread. (In a recently conducted test by a Texas biologist, commercial "enriched" bread was fed to weanling rats for ninety days. All the rats died before the tests were completed.)

• Homemade bread is a simple, healthy combination of natural ingredients—whole grain flour, natural yeast, salt and perhaps some raisins, nuts, or other ingredients to give it texture, flavor, and interest.

• The heavier texture of homemade bread required thorough chewing which helps to clean teeth, stimulate gums, and improve digestion.

• Natural flours give the bread sweetness and goodness not found in the factory-made product (see Chapter 4).

• By the pound, homemade bread is much less expensive than store-bought bread.

• By using natural leavening such as sour dough or yeast, you avoid chemical baking powders.

Making your own bread can be fun for the whole family. To begin, acquire a sack of whole wheat—any type that pleases you. While you're at it, buy some oats, barley, rye or corn to have around for bread variations.

WHOLE GRAIN BREAD

Makes 1 5″ × 10″ loaf
4 cups whole wheat flour, freshly ground
1½ cakes yeast (fresh or dry)
1⅓ cups and 3 tablespoons lukewarm water
2 tablespoons honey
3 tablespoons oil or melted shortening

1 teaspoon salt (optional)
Preheat oven to 375°. Dissolve yeast in 9 tablespoons lukewarm water. Add to it the 1⅓ cups of water, honey, and salt (if desired). Combine with flour. Add the oil or melted shortening. Knead the dough until it is smooth. Shape it into a ball. Cover with cloth and permit to rise for 1 hour. Knead gently once more. Now shape into a loaf and place in greased pan. Let rise again for 1 hour. Bake at 375° for about 50 minutes, or until brown on top. Cost: 41 cents.

SALT-RISING BREAD

This favorite old-time recipe makes 3 loaves.
1 cup corn meal, freshly ground
1 cup scalded milk
3 cups skim milk
½ teaspoon salt
1 tablespoon honey
5 tablespoons oil
10 to 11 cups whole wheat flour, freshly ground
Preheat oven to 350°. Pour scalded milk over corn meal. Permit this to ferment in a warm place for about 12 hours. Mix skim milk, salt, honey, and oil (sesame is great for this) and heat mixture until lukewarm. Stir in three cups of whole wheat flour and add corn mixture. Place in warm place for 2 to 3 hours. Next, stir in 5 more cups whole wheat flour. Knead until smooth, adding another 2 to 3 cups whole wheat flour. Place the dough in three greased pans and allow it to set until it has doubled in bulk. Bake at 350° for 1 hour or until done. Cool and slice. Cost: 87 cents.

QUICK AND EASY BREAD

2 tablespoons honey
4 large eggs
½ cup butter or oil
2 cups whole wheat flour
pinch salt
2 cakes yeast (fresh or dry)
3 tablespoons warm milk or water
Preheat oven to 425°. Beat honey with eggs. Add butter or oil, flour and salt. Dissolve the yeast in warm milk or water. Add these items to the batter and beat it briskly for a couple of minutes. Place in a greased bread loaf pan and let the dough rise in a warm place for about 3 hours. Bake at 425° for about 30 minutes or until brown. Cost: 81 cents.

BOSTON BROWN BREAD

1 cup freshly ground corn meal
1 cup freshly ground rye flour
1 cup graham flour
¾ teaspoon soda
½ teaspoon salt (optional)
2 cups sour milk
¾ cup molasses
1 cup chopped raisins

Combine the meal, flours, soda and salt. In a separate bowl mix liquid ingredients and raisins. Add to dry ingredients. Pour batter into a buttered 2-quart pudding mold and steam for 3 to 4 hours. May be steamed in smaller molds or baking powder cans for 1½ to 2 hours. Cost: $1.04.

FRY BREAD

2 cups whole wheat flour
½ teaspoon salt
3 tablespoons oil
oil for frying
2 teaspoons baking powder
1 egg
½ cup water

Sift flour, baking powder and salt into medium-size bowl. Beat egg in small bowl, stir in oil and water, pour over dry ingredients, stirring until well blended. Turn out onto a lightly floured pastry cloth or board. Knead until smooth. Divide dough in half. Roll out each to a 12-inch square, then cut into 16 3″ depth in a heavy iron saucepan. Heat to about 380° F. Fry squares 2 or 3 at a time and turn often. They will puff up and turn golden. Lift out with slotted spoon, drain on paper towel. Keep warm and hide some for yourself. Cost: 26 cents.

By the way, all breads can be made into rolls. Simply break off chunks of dough and shape them into roll form. Add nuts, raisins, seeds and other goodies to produce a variety of freshly baked good things.

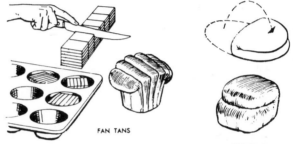

FAN TANS

PARKERHOUSE

THE "RIPE" TEST

KNEADING

PUNCHING DOWN THE DOUGH

Different ways of using flour dough

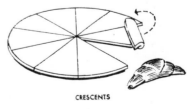

CLOVERLEAF

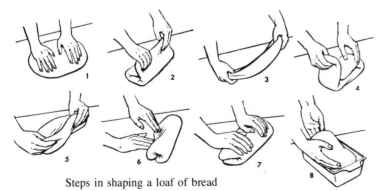

Steps in shaping a loaf of bread

CRESCENTS

The noble spud to your budget's rescue

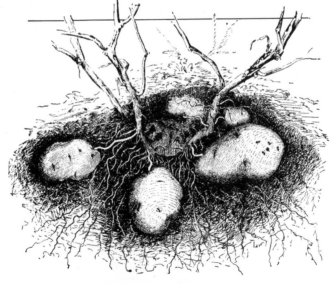

What You'll Learn:

One of the secrets of living well on meals that cost pennies instead of dollars: new ways of preparing low cost foods. Here's all the information you need to make the noble potato a thing of great beauty and special taste.

For the money spent, potatoes give consumers a high return in food value. One medium-sized potato, boiled, baked, or pressure-cooked can supply:

- one-fourth of the Vitamin C recommended for an adult each day,
- worthwhile amounts of thimine and niacin (B vitamins),
- substantial quantities of iron and potassium.

The potato is a healthy food, and it's no more caloric than an apple, orange, or banana. For example, a potato of medium size, boiled or baked provides only about a hundred calories. The commonly added fats, gravies, and sauces are the things that make potatoes an offender for those who must watch their weight as well as their food dollars. Fried potatoes, for example, are the fat cats of the spud tribe. They may be two to four times as high in calories as the same weight of boiled, baked, or pressure-cooked potatoes. So don't blame potatoes for that tight dress or belt. Treat them kindly and plainly and you'll stay healthy and slender.

Buying Potatoes

The best potatoes are firm, smooth and well-shaped. They are free from cuts, blemishes, and decay. Look for potatoes that are reasonably clean so you can see if there are green spots. Avoid this type since the green parts are bitter. If you intend to buy a large quantity at one time, it's very important that you cook and taste a few potatoes from the batch before making your purchase.

Storing Spuds

Potatoes will keep for several months if stored in a cool place with good ventilation. Sort through them and remove any that are cut or blemished. Use these first since they will probably be the first to spoil.

The ideal storage place is in a dark space with a temperature of around 45 to 40°F. A cellar is perfect, but be sure and avoid dampness.

Cooking Potatoes

Don't peel potatoes; if you do you lose the best part, since most of the vitamins and minerals are near the surface. Cook them fast in a small amount of water if you like them boiled; quick cooking saves the nutritional elements. Baking is an even better way to prepare them. Scrub them thoroughly so that the skins can be eaten without fear of dirt.

Eating well on a low budget never need be a drab, colorless, and tasteless way to live. Actually the finest meals in the world are usually the simplest ones—a melted cheese sandwich and German fried potatoes, or a fresh green salad with potatoes au gratin. Potatoes lend themselves well to simple preparation. Here are some great ways to make spuds stand by themselves, even as main dishes.

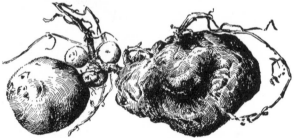

FRIED POTATOES, COUNTRY STYLE

Pare and slice raw potatoes. Heat a little bacon fat or oil in a large iron skillet and add the potatoes. Use about 2 or 3 tablespoons of fat to every 3 cups of sliced potatoes. Season with homemade herb salt and pepper or other spices of your choice. Cover closely and cook over medium heat for 10 or 15 minutes or until the potatoes are brown and crisp on one side. Turn potatoes and brown on the other side. Adding a little onion, crumbled bacon, diced meats will perk them up, but they are delicious just plain. Varies in cost.

FRIED SWEET-SOUR POTATOES

4 slices of bacon
3 cups diced raw potatoes
½ cup chopped onion
½ tablespoon honey
¾ teaspoon herb salt
½ cup water
¼ cup vinegar

Cook bacon in large skillet until crisp. Remove from pan and chop. Using 2 tablespoons of the bacon fat, cook the potatoes over medium heat, without turning, for 15 to 20 minutes, or until they are brown on the bottom. Turn the potatoes with a wide spatula, add onion and cook for 5 more minutes. Sprinkle honey and salt over potatoes, add water, cover and simmer for 15 minutes, or until potatoes are tender. Then remove from heat and pour vinegar over them. Let them stand for about 15 minutes, add chopped bacon and reheat. Cost: 48 cents.

POTATO PUFF

2 cups hot or cold mashed potatoes
3 tablespoons hot milk
1 egg, separated
2 tablespoons butter or margarine, melted
1 teaspoon grated onion
2 tablespoons cut parsley
½ teaspoon salt
pepper

Preheat oven to 375°. To the potato add the hot milk, beaten egg yolk, butter or margarine, onion, parsley, salt and pepper. Mix well. Now beat the egg white until stiff and fold into the potato mixture. Pile lightly into a greased baking dish and bake at 375° for about 35 minutes or until brown. Put the dish under the broiler for a few minutes for a deeper brown. Cost: 22 cents.

POTATO AND MEAT SCALLOP

¾ pound ground beef
1 teaspoon finely chopped onion
1 teaspoon salt
1 tablespoon butter or margarine
1 tablespoon flour 1½ cups milk
2 cups thinly sliced raw potatoes

Preheat oven to 350°. Brown the beef and onion together and add salt. Melt the fat and blend in the flour, gradually adding milk, stirring constantly until it thickens. Place alternate layers of sliced potatoes and beef sauce in a greased baking dish. Cover and bake at 350° for 50 to 60 minutes, removing cover to brown under broiler for the last 5 minutes. For a variation, 2 cups of diced raw ham may be used in place of the beef. Cost: 88 cents.

POTATOES AND HAM WITH CHEESE SAUCE

1 tablespoon butter or margarine
2 tablespoons flour
1 teaspoon salt
pepper
1 cup milk
½ cup grated cheddar cheese
2 cups diced cooked potatoes
1 cup diced cooked ham

Preheat oven to 375°. Melt the shortening and blend in the flour and seasonings. Gradually add the milk, stirring constantly until thickened. Remove from heat and add the cheese. Put alternate layers of potatoes and ham in a greased baking dish and pour the cheese sauce over the top. Cover and bake at 375° for 30 minutes. Remove cover and bake 10 minutes longer to brown the top. Cost: 75 cents.

For more suggestions on how to use potatoes as a main ingredient, order a free copy of *The Potato Lover's Diet Cookbook* by Barbara Gibbons from The Potato Board, 1385 S. Colorado Blvd., Suite 512, Denver, Colorado 80222.

CHAPTER

14

Soybeans:the money-saving meat substitute

What You'll Learn:
Why the Chinese have been using
soybeans for centuries, and how you
can do it too. The economics and
dietetics of soybeans in summary
form.

"The soybean is in so many respects the most valuable of all plant foods."—United States Office of Health Education

About the closest most Americans have come to soybeans is the adding of a little soy sauce to the chow mein at Ah Sing's Oriental Gardens. Good, wasn't it? The soybean is even better when you become familiar with its fantastic versatility. In fact, it's better from many standpoints —economic, nutrition, convenience, and taste.

First, some facts. Soy plants are defined in botanical language as a small erect herb (Glycine soja) that grows in many parts of the world but primarily in China, India, and the United States. The plant itself makes excellent forage for animals, while from the human's point of view, its bean is a source of oil, flour and hundreds of other products.

Here are just a few of the ways in which soy beans are used in the home as food: green soy beans, fresh or frozen; soy flour; soy grits; soy milk powder; soy cheese; soybean sprouts; soy milk; dry soybeans; canned green soybeans; soybean pulp; and the ever-popular soy sauce.

The soybean is the *only* vegetable that yields a complete protein comparable in quality to that of milk, eggs, and meat. Soybeans also consist of about 20 percent unsaturated fats, the most important of these being lecithin, which is also a constituent of eggs, nuts, and seeds. Lecithin has the ability to break up cholesterol and other fatty substances in the body so that they are discouraged from forming plaques within the artery walls.

Soy Protein Manufacturers

Company	Product Name	Product Form
Loma Linda Foods	Fibrotein and TVP. (Textured vegetable protein)	Dry and canned soy protein
Worthington Foods (Miles Laboratory)	Fibrotein	Dry, frozen, and canned soy protein
General Mills, Inc.	Bacos	Dry soy protein
	Bontrae	Frozen soy protein
Archer Daniels	T.V.P.	Dry soy protein
*A. E. Stanley Co.	Mira-Tex	
*Central Soya	Promosoy	
*Farm-Mar-Co	Ultra-Soy	
*H. B. Taylor Co.	Textra Soy	
*Ralston Purina	Edi-Pro	
*Swift and Co.	Texgran	

* Companies that make several soy protein ingredients but do not market any as "finished" products to use in recipes.

Proximate Analysis of Soy Flour

Composition	Full-fat soy flour	Defatted soy flour
	per cent	per cent
Protein	41.0	50.5
Fat	20.5	1.5
Carbohydrates	25.2	34.2

Cost

Besides their nutritional value, the most outstanding feature of soybeans is their low cost both in terms of price per pound and price per unit of food value. Take a look at this comparison of soy beans and beef:

Mrs. Smith Paid:		
$7.40		$7.40
for		for
4½ pounds		25 pounds
Beef		**Soybeans**
(rib roast)		

Mrs. Smith Received:		
from beef		*from soybeans*
6	SERVINGS	150
13	DAYS PROTEIN	180
355	TOTAL PROTEIN (gm)	4,540
5,659	CALORIES	37,569
204	CALCIUM (mg)	25,756
3,841	PHOSPHORUS (mg)	66,511
53	IRON (mg)	908
0	VITAMIN A (I.U.)	15,890
2	VITAMIN B1 (mg)	121
3	VITAMIN B2 (mg)	35

By using soybeans, then, you get *25 times* more servings (6 of beef to 150 of soybeans!), *13 times* more protein, about *seven times* the calories, and very big jolts of valuable vitamins. Think of how much better your entire family will feel when they add soybeans to their daily diet. You'll be able to tell the difference in a matter of days. In addition, you'll need a haybaler to wire up the dollars you'll save by not buying beef.

Many cookbooks neglect this important food, so we'll make up the deficit right now.

SOY BURGERS

Soak 1 cup dry soybeans overnight and cook covered over low heat for 2 to 3 hours or until tender. Drain off liquid (stock can be used for soups), mash very well, and add any of the following, experimenting with different amounts and combinations: chopped onions, chopped (fine) garlic, celery, sesame seeds, sunflower seeds, chopped peanuts, chopped green pepper, cooked brown rice or bulgar wheat, chopped fresh parsley.

Make into patties and broil until browned. Serve on whole wheat buns or bread with homemade mayonnaise and plenty of alfalfa sprouts. Cost: 40 cents for 2.

SOYBEAN SOUFFLÉ

3 cups soybean pulp
3 eggs, separated
1 tablespoon chopped onion
2 tablespoons chopped parsley
salt and pepper to taste

To make the pulp, drain cooked soybeans. Put through a food press or sieve; or mash thoroughly. This paste may be stored in the refrigerator and used as needed.

Preheat oven to 325°. Beat the yolks of the eggs and add them to the other ingredients. Then fold this mixture into the well-beaten egg whites, and pour into a greased baking dish. Bake at 325° for 30 minutes or until set. Serve at once. Cost: 57 cents.

HONEY SOY DRINK

1 cup soy milk powder
4 cups water
1 tablespoon honey

Mix powder with a small amount of water until smooth. Blend into remaining water. Let stand 2 hours. Cook 20 minutes in double boiler. Strain. Flavor with honey and salt. Keep refrigerated. Cost: 32 cents.

For more complete information on the various ways that soybeans can be used to help you feed your family better, write to the U.S. Department of Agriculture, Washington, D.C. 20250. Also, write to El Molino Mills, 3060 W. Valley Blvd., Alhambra, California 91803 and ask for a copy of *Tested Recipes from El Molino Kitchens*. It costs $1.00 (California residents add the sales tax, please).

MPF:
the multi-purpose
food

*"Is It Any Wonder I Am Getting the
Reputation of Being a Dyspeptic?"*

What You'll Learn:
All about the little-known product
MPF—what it is and how to use it to
provide all the protein you need for
about twenty-five cents a day.

If you don't read any other chapter of this book, read this one. It could be the breakthrough you have been looking for to save money and eat better simultaneously. What's the commotion about? It's MPF, Multi-Purpose Food, the fabulously nutritious product that costs so little you can afford to eat it at every meal, growing more and more healthy thereby.

The History of MPF

Some years back, a man with a large and generous heart, Los Angeles restauranteur Clifford Clinton,* donated money to research for developing new food products. As a result of Clinton's donations, MPF was developed by Dr. Henry Borsook, a professor of biochemistry at the California Institute of Technology in Pasadena. Borsook's objective had been to develop a product that was high in quality protein and fortified with essential minerals and vitamins but low in cost and bulk. He achieved his goal: just six ounces of MPF provides *all* of the minimum daily requirement for twelve essential vitamins and minerals and *all* the recommended daily adult allowance for protein.

Since 1946, MPF has been distributed in more than 125 countries to combat hunger, protein deficiencies, and malnutrition. Surely it's time this valuable and versatile product became a household staple in the United States.

But What Is MPF?

When you open a can of MPF, you'll find a brown, flour-like substance. Taste it; you'll probably compare it with rich, nutty whole wheat cereal. It's

*Incidentally, Clinton was a benefactor who fed many a hungry man during the Great Depression. His restaurants had a policy whereby if a diner could not afford to pay, he didn't have to. Others more fortunate donated money to carry on this fine program.

pre-cooked and can be eaten dry, stirred into liquids such as vegetable or fruit juices and soups, or it can be used as an ingredient in almost any dish you are accustomed to preparing. When MPF is added to something, the nutritive value of the dish is immediately increased.

Those who have tried MPF find it very satisfying. A small amount eaten at any meal helps that particular meal to satisfy you longer. You'll also have more energy all day. MPF is a real food, not a health-food fad or a medicine.

One pound of MPF makes from two to three pounds of prepared food. For example, you can add it to juices in the ratio of one part MPF to two parts juice. Thus you obtain a total of three parts delicious, healthful, and nutritious food.

On the opposite page is an extract from a recent bulletin published by Meals for Millions, the organization in charge of distributing MPF.

The Economics of MPF

MPF is so cheap you'll wonder why you have been spending a fortune on beef and pork all these years. As this book goes to press, a four-pound can of MPF costs $4.50, or about $1.13 per pound. Compare that with what you currently spend for beef with bones and fat. And keep in mind that 50 percent of the MPF you buy is pure protein in easily usable form. Since you only need six ounces of this marvelous food to get all the protein, minerals, and vitamins you need, your total cost per day for MPF can be about 42 cents. Now, adding simple carbohydrates like whole wheat at 13 cents a pound, plus some butter at 80 cents a pound, and some fruits and vegetables, you can eat for less than a dollar a day.

Even if you are a meat lover, you'll find that MPF can be added to things like meat loaf, meat balls, chili con carne, spaghetti sauce and hamburgers to stretch

MPF Nutrients Chart

Ingredients

Toasted soy protein, calcium carbonate, sodium ascorbate, tocopherol acetate (vitamin E), vitamin A palmitate, niacinamide, cyanocobalamin (vitamin B^{12}), pyridoxine hydrochloride (vitamin B^6), riboflavin, vitamin D and potassium iodide.

Special Dietary Information

Two ozs. (56.7 grams) dry weight of MPF provide 33½% of the recommended daily allowance (RDA) for 12 essential vitamins and minerals and 43% of the recommended daily allowance for protein of an adult male of 154 lbs. (70 kg) weight.

	Min. in 2 oz.	%MDR*	%RDA**
Protein	28.00 gm.	—	43.0
Vitamin A	1667.00 I. U.	41.5	33.3
Vitamin D	167.00 I.U.	41.5	—
Vitamin C	20.00 mg.	66.7	33.3
Vitamin E	10.00 I.U.	***	33.3
Thiamine	0.50 mg.	50.0	33.3
Riboflavin	0.60 mg.	50.0	33.3
Niacin	6.00 mg.	60.0	33.3
Vitamin B^6	0.67 mg.	—	33.3
Vitamin B^{12}	1.70 mcg.	—	33.3
Iron	3.40 mg.	33.3	33.3
Iodine	0.05 mg.	47.0	33.3
Calcium	300.00 mg.	40.0	33.3
Phosphorus	300.00 mg.	40.0	33.3

Approximate Composition

Protein (N x 6.25)	**50.0%**
Available Carbohydrates	15.5%
Non-available Carbohydrates	15.5%
Ash (Mineral)	6.8%
Fat (by Acid hydrolysis)	2.2%
Moisture	10.0%

Available Calories in 2 ozs.   *–150*

Essential Amino Acids

Lysine	1.8 Gms.
Phenylanine	1.5 Gms.
Tryptophane	0.4 Gms.
†Methionine/Cystine	0.9 Gms.
Threonine	1.1 Gms.
Leucine	2.2 Gms.
Iso-Leucine	1.6 Gms.
Valine	1.5 Gms.

Special Note About the Protein in MPF:

This protein is prepared under carefully controlled conditions which remove the typical soy flavor, inactivate the enzymes and enzyme inhibitors without damaging the heat-sensitive amino acids. The result—a delicately toasted product, high in protein, exceptionally stable and of good nutritional quality. It violates no known dietary or religious precepts.

Carbohydrates:

The carboyhydrates in MPF consist principally of soluble sugars, including sucrose, stachyose and raffinose; insoluble products such as cellulose, hemicellulose, pentosans and lignin. Approximately 50% of the carbohydrates in MPF are digestible.

Minerals:

MPF contains approximately 2.5% of potassium, 0.5% calcium, 0.5% phosphorus and 0.3% sodium.

Lipids:

In addition to fat, MPF contains small percentages of phosphatides (lecithin) and sterols (no cholesterol).

*MDR refers to Minimum Daily Requirements as established by the U.S. Food and Drug Administration.

**Percentages are based on the RDA for a 22 year old male. Percentages may be different for the other ages or sex.

***The MDR has not been established yet.

†Cystine can provide part of the Methionine requirement.

their inherent goodness. Here's a typical example of how MPF can stretch your food dollars with regard to meat. Let's say you pay $1.00 a pound for fairly lean ground beef. Now add eight ounces of MPF dissolved in eight ounces of plain water. (Many food chains, especially those who sell mainly hamburgers, add soya flour or MPF to their ground meat. This reduces costs and makes the meat taste better.) You now have two pounds of ground beef for a total cost of $1.56. Dividing by two, you have reduced the cost of your beef to about 78 cents a pound while at the same time substantially increasing its food value. (MPF is actually higher in protein than beef.)

How to Use MPF

MPF can be added dry to anything you wish, but it is best to moisten MPF with an equal volume of water and let the mixture hydrate for about ten minutes before using. Then add ¼ cup of the hydrated MPF to every full cup of flour, dry mix, dry meal, dry cereal, prepared hot cereal, prepared soup or broth, ground meat, or prepared mashed vegetables you happen to be using.

Simply blend the hydrated MPF mix with the other food until it is thoroughly distributed. Then proceed to prepare the food as usual. No other change in procedure is necessary.

By the way, mothers of young children take note. MPF blended or cooked with liquids may be used as an infant food, either alone or in combination with other baby foods. By increasing the quantity of water, it can be served as a gruel or fed from the bottle.

Here, now, are some recipes suited to your dollar-a-day budget adapted from the cookbook assembled by the Meals for Millions people.

For more information on receiving MPF, write to Meals for Millions Foundation, 1800 Olympic Blvd., P.O. Box 1666, Santa Monica, Ca. 90406.

Bill Kaysing

Recipes With MPF

MEAT LOAF

½ pound ground beef
½ pound ground pork
⅓ cup MPF
⅔ cup liquid (milk or broth)
½ onion, chopped
1 teaspoon Worcestershire sauce
¼ teaspoon black pepper
1 large egg
Salt to taste

Preheat oven to 350°. Soak MPF in liquid. Combine mixture with remaining ingredients. Mix well. Place meat mixture in greased loaf pan. Bake about one hour or until done at 350°. Allow loaf to absorb juices for about 5 minutes before removing from pan. For variety, add different seasonings. Add 3 tablespoons chopped celery and/or green pepper. Pour off drippings, blend with 1 can tomato or mushroom soup and simmer 5 minutes. Serve hot sauce with loaf. Makes about 6 servings. (Cost: $1.11)

HAMBURGER PIE

1 pound ground beef
1 onion, chopped
⅛ teaspoon pepper
2½ cups green beans
⅔ cup MPF
5 medium potatoes, cooked
½ cup warm milk
1 egg beaten
salt and red paprika to taste
1 can tomato soup (10½ oz.)

Preheat oven to 350°. Cook onion in hot fat till golden; add meat and seasonings; brown. Drain beans, use ¾ cup liquid to soak MPF. Add MPF mixture, green beans and soup to meat; pour into greased 2 quart casserole. Mash the potatoes; add the milk, egg and salt. Spoon mounds over meat. Sprinkle with paprika. Bake in moderate oven for 30 minutes. Makes 7 servings. (Cost: $2.10 or 30 cents per serving)

CHILI CON CARNE

1 pound dried red beans
3 tablespoons shortening
1 onion, minced
1 pound ground beef
1 bay leaf
2 tablespoons chili powder
⅛ to ¼ teaspoon cumin
⅔ cup MPF in 1 cup water
1 can tomatoes (1 lb. 13 oz.)
Salt to taste

Wash beans and soak overnight. Cover with water, salt, and cook until tender. Brown onion and meat in hot shortening. Add the tomatoes and seasonings. Simmer two hours, adding water if necessary. Add MPF mixture and cooked beans to the meat sauce, salt and pepper to taste, and simmer another 10 minutes. Makes 10 to 12 cups. (Cost: $2.10)

Recipes from around the world

What You'll Learn:
That a variety of taste-tempting,
low-cost foods are available at your
local ethnic specialty grocery. How to
go the foreign-food route to eat better
for less. Recipes and specifics.

Most American communities have at least one small ethnic grocery store, and the larger cities often have a store for each racial and ethnic group—Mexican, Chinese, Italian, Japanese, and so forth. Even tiny towns often have a store that caters to a specific segment of the population. For example, there's a store in Soledad, California, a village just off the north-south freeway, that sells every conceivable Mexican foodstuff and fresh hot tamales that I can't pass up, even on the most urgent trip up or down the state. So look around your own community. Check the phone book under grocers; if you see a Juanita's Grocery or a Pasquale's Produce, drop in soon. Buy things like:

- Tortillas, 25¢/dozen
- Tamales, 40¢ and up (but you can make your own)
- Masa (corn flour), 20¢/lb.
- Dried Hot Chilis, 85¢/lb.
- Mexican Cheese, $1.25/lb.
- Pinto Beans, 50¢/lb.

The recipes that follow are intended to introduce you to the world's store of culinary skill and imagination. Most of the dishes presented do not require specialty foods, and can be prepared from the foods you would ordinarily have on hand in your pantry and storage bins.

Mexican Food

Mexico, despite the tourist advertising you read, is a very poor country. The majority of its population lives only slightly above subsistence level. This has always been so and conditions change slowly, so the average Mexican has had lots of time to learn how to make very plain and simple foods taste delicious. The proliferation of Mexican restaurants in the United States attests to the popularity of Mexican food. Of all ethnic foods, I believe that Mexican foods offer the most taste for the least amount of money. Here are several Mexican dishes that anyone can make.

MEXICAN HASH

2 large onions, chopped
1 cup diced cooked beef or lamb
1 teaspoon salt
2 cups cooked kidney beans
¼ cup bacon fat
2 teaspoons chili powder
¼ teaspoon pepper
2 cups shredded lettuce

Sauté chopped onions in bacon fat, add chili, beef, salt, pepper, and beans. Cook slowly for 15 minutes, stirring occasionally. Serve on deep platter with shredded lettuce piled in mound in center. *Salsa** optional but good. Serves 4. Cost: $1.12.

HUEVOS RANCHEROS

Make a hot ranchero sauce by combining some tomato sauce with sautéed onions, peppers (green or red), and a bit of chili powder. This is a freewheeling type of sauce; you can toss into it anything with a Mexican bent. When bubbling, break some eggs into the sauce and poach them. Serve with hot buttered tortillas. Cost: 60 cents.

* Salsa usually consists of chopped tomatoes, onions and green chilis in any desired proportions.

REFRIED BEANS

Soak some pinto or red kidney beans overnight. Rinse and check for rocks. Simmer until tender. Drain, combine with sautéed onions, as many green chilis as you can afford, and a fair quantity of home-rendered lard. Now they can be reheated (refried) at any time as a delicious side dish to any other Mexican treat. Cost varies with bean prices.

TACOS

A close friend of mine solved the problem of ensuring a good diet for his eight children. He simply let them go wild on infinite variations of tacos. The tortillas are usually quite cheap and the fillings can be anything from the classic ground beef, lettuce, cheese and sauce to beans, rice, chopped crisp vegetables of all kinds and homemade dressings.

I've often eaten at this household, and never got the same type of taco twice; I was never disappointed.

Try this low-cost, healthy way to feeding a bunch. Here's the basic taco recipe...the fillings can be varied to suit what you have or what you like: Heat tortillas in frying pan in hot oil. Fold over and fry until as crisp as desired. Then fill with meat, cheese, beans, rice, chilis, lettuce, tomatoes, olives, avocados, any or all. Top with hot sauce if desired.

CHOWDERS

So you think there are only two kinds of clam chowder —Boston, the white kind, and Manhattan, with the tomato base? Well, my friend from Baja reports that down on his peninsula chowder is made from just about anything that swims: codfish, mussle, goose barnacle, oyster, sea bass, corn and seafood, and shrimp.

Italian Food

As food costs rise, the Italian genius for making blah pasta taste divine with slow simmered sauces becomes ever more valuable. You can develop this skill in your own kitchen. But Italian cooking involves more than just pasta. Here's an introductory assortment of recipes.

ITALIAN GNOCCHI

2 cups milk
½ cup farina
1 teaspoon salt
2 tablespoons butter
1 cup grated cheese
2 eggs
grated cheese (additional)

Preheat oven to 375°. Scald the milk in the top of a double boiler. Gradually add the farina; cook and stir until the mixture thickens. Add the salt and butter and continue to cook for 20 minutes, stirring occasionally. Remove from the heat; add the cheese, and stir until the mixture is free from lumps. Separate the eggs; beat the yolks until thick and lemon-colored; and add to the farina mixture. Fold in the egg whites, whipped stiff; and transfer mixture to a shallow loaf-cake pan, rinsed with cold water. Cool, chill, and cut in squares, rounds, or fancy shapes with sandwich cutters. Transfer to a shallow pan rubbed plentifully with butter, sprinkle with the additional cheese. Bake in a hot oven, 375°, for 15 minutes, or until brown all over. Cost: 96 cents.

ITALIAN SPAGHETTI

1 pound uncooked spaghetti
½ cup butter
3 cloves garlic or
    ½ cup chopped raw onion
½ pound chopped raw beef
1 can tomato paste
water
¾ teaspoon salt
⅛ teaspoon pepper
Parmesan cheese
Add oregano, thyme or any other appropriate spices.

Boil the spaghetti until tender but not mushy in salted water. Drain. While the spaghetti is cooking put the butter in a small heavy frying pan; add the garlic or onion if used, and sauté until yellow in the butter. Then add the meat and sauté, stirring with a fork until lightly browned. Combine the tomato paste with an equal amount of water; add to the meat mixture and simmer until thick; season with the salt and pepper. Allow 30 minutes to make this sauce. Pour over the spaghetti and top with plenty of Parmesan cheese. Cost: $1.30.

ITALIAN EGGPLANT

1 medium-sized eggplant
flour, whole wheat
2 eggs
¼ cup grated Parmesan
salt and pepper
2 tablespoons minced parsley
margarine
2 cups canned tomatoes
pinch of oregano, sage, thyme or basil

Preheat oven to 350°. Slice the eggplant in quarter-inch slices. It is not necessary to peel it or to squeeze out the juice. Dip each slice in flour. Slightly beat the eggs and add the cheese, one-fourth teaspoon black pepper, one-half teaspoon salt, and the parsley. Dip the floured slices in this mixture and fry first on one side then on the other until browned in margarine, just enough to barely cover the bottom of a heavy frying pan. Remove the eggplant. There should be two tablespoons of margarine left in the pan. Add the tomato and simmer ten minutes. Then place the eggplant in layers in buttered baking dish and pour the tomato mixture over it. Bake for 20 minutes at 350°. Cost: $1.10.

Chinese Food

The Chinese have the oldest continuous culture on earth, so it's no surprise that their culinary prowess transcends all others. Nor is it surprising that they've discovered how to maintain good health, top taste, mealtime interest all on a foundation of extremely basic food elements. Practically everything you enjoy in a Chinese restaurant is inexpensive. What meat is used is treated as if it were the crown jewels it now resembles in price. Learn to make your own egg foo yung and chow mein; you'll be pleasantly surprised at how easy it is.

SHRIMP EGG FOO YUNG

2 teaspoons cornstarch
¼ cup water
1 chicken bouillon cube
2 teaspoons soy sauce
¼ teaspoon salt
1 tablespoon oil
1 teaspoon vinegar
½ teaspoon honey
6 eggs
1 cup diced shrimp, fresh or frozen
1 cup bean sprouts (your own homegrown sprouts)
½ cup chopped green onion
Blend cornstarch with water in a pan until smooth, add chicken cube, soy sauce, vinegar, and honey. Cook, stirring constantly until sauce thickens. Keep warm on low heat. Beat eggs in bowl, stir in shrimp, onion, sprouts, and salt. Heat a large old cast iron skillet until water drops dance on its surface. Lightly grease with oil. Pour in egg mixture about 3 tablespoons a time. Bake until set and turn. Serve with sauce on top. Cost: $1.81.

FLYING GOOSE CHOW MEIN

This summer, we all stayed on our boat, an old Coast Guard cutter called the *Flying Goose*. We made lots of Chinese food because it's cheap and healthy. This was one of our favorites:

Cut up and stir fry (quickly fry in oil) a lot of different vegetables, starting with the toughest ones first—celery and onions—and ending with the tenderest—sprouts and bok choy leaves. In a separate pot, boil up a big quantity of chow mein noodles. These can be purchased in fresh or dry form. Drain noodles, add some sesame oil and mix. Now serve the vegetables over the noodles and pass the soy sauce. Optional, pass the Thailand Fish Soy, which is super great!

SOYBEANS SHANGHAI

1 cup cooked soybeans (best to soak overnight, then simmer until tender)
½ cup of water in which soybeans were cooked.
½ cup tomatoes, diced
½ cup celery or bok choy, sliced
½ onion, grated
¼ cup soy sauce
Simmer ingredients 15 minutes; serve hot with crisp noodles or wonton. Cost: 40 cents.

Japanese Food

Similar in many ways to Chinese, Japanese cookery is strong on seafood. After all, besides rice, seafood is the only major food resource in Japan. Once you've tried "raw fish" (actually it is "cooked" by enzyme action), you'll probably, to continue the imagery, be hooked for life.

SUSHI (JAPANESE RAW FISH)

Cube raw fish, marinate in lemon or lime juice one hour or more. Serve chilled with soy sauce or hot mustard and tomato sauce combination. Simple, delicious, nutritious, inexpensive. Cost: 75 cents to $1.00 for 16 pieces.

German Food

The thoughts of German cooking often elicits an image of rather heavy food. This is not entirely accurate. The peasant culture has dreamed up some highly creative dishes—for instance, shredded red cabbage flavored with caraway seeds and other spices. This imaginative treatment transforms the cabbage into pure vegetary ambrosia, delicious hot or cold. Best of all, it's super cheap. So look for the characteristic dishes in a good German cookbook. Here's a selection I learned by heart from my mother.

POTATO AND HERRING CASSEROLE

1 large onion
6 cups raw potatoes
¼ teaspoon pepper
3 tablespoons butter
1 can herring
½ pint cream

Preheat oven to 350°. Sauté onion until soft in 2 tablespoons of butter. Layer potatoes, herring and onion in a large greased baking dish. Begin and end with the spuds. Sprinkle pepper between layers. Pour cream over potatoes. Dot top with remaining butter. Bake covered at 350° for 30 minutes. Remove cover and bake 30 minutes more until bubbling and golden brown. Cost: $1.00

RED CABBAGE

The Chinese serve red cabbage mixed with green peppers and vinegar. But the Germans offer us this delicious combination. It's great hot, and just as good next day served as a cold relish.

1 head red cabbage
3 slices bacon
2 tablespoons onion, chopped
2 apples, cored and sliced thin
2 tablespoons flour
½ cup diluted vinegar or red wine
2 tablespoons honey
caraway seeds

Trim cabbage, cut into sections, remove core, shred and soak in cold water. Cut bacon into small pieces and sauté over low heat. Sauté chopped onion in the hot bacon fat. Simmer cabbage with ¼ teaspoon salt if necessary. Stir pot and simmer for about 1½ hours. Add water if necessary and caraway seeds to suit. Dissolve flour in diluted vinegar or red wine, stir in honey and add to cabbage mixture. Simmer 10 or 15 minutes longer. Serves 4. Cost: 80 cents.

SAUERKRAUT

Shred all that leftover cabbage, sprinkle a little salt between layers as you place them in a large crock, and weigh it down with a piece of clean wood and a rock. The cabbage will ferment on its own. Just store it in a cool place until you need it. Make a lot; it's great with spare ribs, sausages, and German fried potatoes.

French Food

Do you know how the doughty, independent French have survived two world wars, Charles de Gaulle, and a declining share of world markets? It's simple—an unusually large proportion of French families have backyard gardens from which to obtain staples. The vegetables and fruits they grow, and the goats that some have for milk provide the rudiments of all meals. These items plus some wine, the ubiquitous and rightfully famous French bread, and an occasional rack of lamb would keep any family happy. (We might all take this to heart and plant some vegetable seeds instead of lawn come spring.)

Here are two recipes so French that they are almost indecently delicious.

BÉARNAISE SAUCE

3 tablespoons cider vineagr
3 tablespoons tarragon vinegar
1 small onion, minced
3 egg yolks
½ cup butter
½ teaspoon salt
⅛ teaspoon cayenne

Combine the vinegars; add the onion and cook for three minutes over a moderate heat. Strain onions out and pour the liquor into the egg yolks, well beaten. Transfer mixture to the top of a double boiler. Cook and stir over a low heat until the mixture thickens. Then add the butter a teaspoonful at a time, working in each portion before more is added. Season with the salt and cayenne and serve immediately over broiled meat or fish. Also delicious over egg dishes. Cost: 50 cents.

STEAMED FRENCH BREAD PUDDING

1 small loaf bread or 3 cups (solidly packed) bread cubes
½ cup butter
½ cup honey
2 eggs
½ teaspoon nutmeg
grated rind of 1 orange
½ teaspoon baking powder
⅓ cup chopped raisins
2 tablespoons shredded citron (optional)

The bread should be cut or broken into very small pieces. In a bowl, pour enough hot water over the bread to barely cover it. Cool, drain, and press as much water out as possible with a fork. In a large bowl cream the butter with the sugar and the egg yolks, slightly beaten. Add the bread, nutmeg, orange rind, baking powder, raisins, and citron. Fold in the egg whites, stiffly whipped. Transfer to a mold rubbed with butter. Cover tightly, place on a trivet in a pot with 1 inch of boiling water. Cover kettle closely, lower heat, and steam for two hours. Unmold and serve with hard or pineapple sauce. Cost: 97 cents.

Middle Eastern Dishes

A teacher friend of mine who had spent some years in Turkey said that the American dollar went further there than in any other place in Europe. That, of course, means that the standard of living in Turkey is low and that foods are, of necessity, cheap and filling. Further, people strive mightily to make the most of what little they have. All of this leads to some interesting recipes for fundamental foods.

CONSTANTINOPLE PEPPER POT

½ cup garbanzo beans (cow peas)
1½ quarts well-seasoned soup stock
¾ pound fresh or pickled tripe
juice of ½ lemon
salt and pepper
1 clove garlic, crushed, or 2 tablespoons minced onion
½ tablespoon flour
1 tablespoon butter
1 egg
boiled rice
Soak the cow-peas overnight. Drain and add to the stock, which should be boiling. Cook rapidly for an hour. In the meantime, cover the tripe with cold water and bring to boiling point. Then scrape it and cut into 1 inch strips or cubes. Add the tripe and garlic to the stock, replenishing the stock as it evaporates. Simmer two hours. Season to taste with salt and pepper. Cream together the butter, flour, and lemon juice. Stir carefully into the soup and boil a minute or two, stirring constantly. Beat the egg lightly with a bit of hot soup and add. Serve at once with large spoonsful of boiled rice in the center of each plate. Cost: 85 cents.

PILAF

Takes the place of potatoes and is better than anything you buy in a box.

1 cup barley (or any other grain)
4 tablespoons butter or margarine
1 large onion
chicken broth (preferably homemade)
Cook barley in a large amount of boiling water until tender and drain. Sauté onion in butter until soft, stir in chicken broth. Add barley, toss to mix well. Cover. Heat very slowly until heated through. A low cost, tasty dish you'll serve often. Rice and other grains can be adorned in the same way. Serves 2 generously. Cost: 35 cents.

Soul Food

In the old days, the masters of plantations ate high on the hog and gave their slaves the leftovers. Necessity being the mother of invention, all those scraps developed into some tasty dishes passed down and refined through the generations.

SOUL SUCCOTASH

1 cup dried baby lima beans, soaked overnight in refrigerator
3 cups water
1 teaspoon salt
1 can (#303) stewed tomatoes or 2 cups tomatoes with juice
¼ teaspoon thyme
2 small bay leaves
1 tablespoon chopped green peppers
1 tablespoon bacon fat
1 cup corn kernels
Place in a large pot all of the ingredients, except the corn. Bring to a boil. Cover pot. Lower heat. Simmer 1½ hours. Add more water, if needed. Water should cover beans and vegetables throughout cooking time. Add corn. Cover. Cook another 25 minutes. Correct seasoning. Serves 4. Cost: 76 cents.

NAVY (PEA) BEANS 'N SAUSAGES

1 cup pea beans (dried)
1 pound pork neck bones (smoked)
4-6 pork sausages
¼ pound salt pork, diced
1-2 medium onions, chopped
2 cups stewed tomatoes
1 bay leaf
½ teaspoon salt
¼ teaspoon black pepper
3 cups water
Soak beans overnight in refrigerator. Drain and discard any that are discolored. Parboil neck bones for 30 minutes. Drain. Brown sausages and salt pork in a heavy frying pan. Add onions and cook until yellow. In a large pot place all of the ingredients. Cover and simmer over a low flame for 2-2½ hours or until beans are tender. Add water, as needed. This dish is on the soupy rather than the dry side. Serve over rice. Serves 4. Cost: $1.55.

This recipe is so simple, you'll laugh when you read the directions, so start chuckling.

WILD WILLY'S CORNCAKES

Grind up a cup or so of your whole grain corn to a reasonably fine texture. Mix into a thin batter with water, milk and even a nice fresh organic egg or two. But water alone will do if you're going the poor-man route. Heat your griddle until a drop of water dances on the surface. Grease the griddle with whatever you have available—butter, oil, chicken fat, or bear grease. Now pour the batter out so it fairly crackles as it solidifies. It should be a quick process; otherwise you'll get soggy little cakes that will just sit there with a mournful expression. A well-cooked corncake is crisp on the edges. They are delicious with butter and whatever else you have available—honey, chopped fresh fruit, ground dates. Be imaginative; roll them up with sour cream and slices of melon or cottage cheese and bits of ham or bacon. They make a good substitute for tortillas, too. Great food any time—morning, noon, or night.

Indian Food

People in India, despite news bulletins of disaster and famine, *do* get something to eat once in a while. And here is an example of what they do with it. You'll find the distinctively Indian curry flavor a delicious change. An easy way to add variety to your diet.

INDIAN SAUCE

1½ tablespoons butter
1½ tablespoons flour
1 cup soup stock
1 teaspoon curry powder
½ tablespoon minced onion
grated rind of ¼ lemon
½ cup chopped tomato
a bit of bay leaf
few grains salt
few grains cayenne

Melt the butter. Add the flour and gradually the soup stock. Stir in the curry powder, mixed with a teaspoonful of cold water. Add the remaining ingredients to the sauce and season to taste. Simmer about ten minutes. Cost: 25 cents.

CURRY SOUP

½ pound lentils
2 pints water or stock
2 large onions
1 turnip
2 tablespoons butter
1 tablespoon flour, whole wheat
2 teaspoons curry powder
2 teaspoons chutney
salt and pepper optional

Fry sliced vegetables in butter until brown. Add lentils and water or stock. Simmer one hour; then sieve or blend to smoothness. Return to pan and re-heat with flour and seasonings. Serve with chapatties (Indian tortilla-like bread) or crackers. Cost: 55 cents.

Russian Food

Did you know that some peasants in northern Siberia exist all winter on a diet of pine or piñon nuts? Others, slightly southward, have a bit more variety, and when you get down to civilization, you might run into something like these piroushki, as traditional as the May Day Parade in front of the Kremlin.

RUSSIAN PIROUSHKI

Preheat oven to 375°. Follow a recipe for Baking Powder Biscuits.

Roll to ⅛ inch in thickness. Dot the dough with 4 tablespoons additional butter; fold over in thirds and press the edges together. Roll to ¼ inch in thickness and cut into 2-inch rounds using a biscuit cutter. Combine 1½ cups chopped left-over meat with gravy or white cream sauce to moisten and place a tablespoon of the mixture on half of the biscuit rounds. Cover each with a second round of the plain dough, moistening the edges and pressing them lightly together. Transfer to a shallow pan rubbed with butter, and brush the tops with an egg yolk, slightly beaten. Bake in 375° oven for 20 minutes, or until puffy and brown on top. Serve hot, plain, or with gravy or cream sauce. Makes 24. Cost: $1.00.

Swiss Food

Switzerland is famous for more than its beautiful scenery. The Swiss are particularly imaginative when it comes to dairy food.

SWISS CHEESE BISCUITS

(can be made with other kinds of cheese like Cheddar for example)

2 cups whole wheat flour
4 teaspoons baking powder
½ teaspoon salt
6 tablespoons butter
2 egg yolks or one whole egg
⅔ cup milk
½ cup grated Swiss (or other) cheese

Preheat oven to 425°. Sift the dry ingredients together and cut in the butter with the back and edge of a spoon until the consistency of coarse cornmeal. In another bowl beat the egg yolks and add the milk; mix and add to the first mixture and mix until blended. Transfer to board dusted with flour and knead for a few seconds. Roll or pat out to ⅛ inch in thickness and sprinkle half of the dough with the grated cheese. Fold the dough over and shape with a small biscuit cutter. Transfer to a shallow pan or baking sheet rubbed with butter. Brush the tops of the biscuits with a little milk and sprinkle with a little additional cheese. Bake in a very hot oven 400-425° for 15 minutes, or until puffy and brown. Cost: 85 cents.

Danish Food

Danish pastries and cheese dishes are world-famous.

DANISH APFELSKIVER

1½ cups whole wheat flour
2 teaspoons baking powder
½ teaspoon salt
3 eggs, separated
1 cup milk
3 tablespoons melted butter

Preheat oven to 375°. Sift the dry ingredients. In a separate bowl, beat the egg yolks and add the milk. Stir into the flour mixture; add the butter and egg whites, whipped stiff. Transfer to hot Apfelskiver pans rubbed with butter or use tiny round muffin pans. Bake about 20 minutes at 375°. Adorn with applesauce. Cost: 49 cents.

RICH CHEESE SAUCE

4 tablespoons butter
3 tablespoons whole wheat flour
½ teaspoon salt
⅛ teaspoon paprika
1½ cups milk
1 cup finely chopped sharp cheddar

Melt the butter, add the flour and seasonings, and blend. Gradually add the milk. Cook and stir until the sauce thickens. Add the cheese. Place over hot water, or in the top of a double boiler and cook and stir until the cheese melts. Cost: 54 cents.

Scottish Food

The independent Scottish people draw much of their sustenance from rough and nutritious grains. Here are a couple of appropriate recipes.

PLAIN SCONES

2 cups whole wheat flour
1 tablespoon honey
¼ teaspoon baking soda
2½ teaspoons baking powder
½ teaspoon salt
5 tablespoons butter
¾ cup buttermilk or sour milk

Preheat oven to 400°. Sift the dry ingredients together. Cut in the butter until the consistency of coarse cornmeal. Add the buttermilk, blend the mixture together, and divide into two portions. Transfer to a board dusted with flour; and roll each portion into a round shape, ¼ inch in thickness. Cut each round in quarters, and transfer to a baking sheet generously rubbed with butter. Bake at 400° for 15 minutes, or until brown on top. Split; spread with butter, and serve hot with marmalade or jam. Cost: 34 cents.

SCOTCH SHORTBREAD

2 cups whole wheat flour
½ teaspoon salt
½ teaspoon nutmeg
¾ cup butter
½ cup honey

Preheat oven to 350°. Sift together the flour, salt, and nutmeg. Rub the butter into dry ingredients with the finger tips; then work in the honey, continually kneading and working until the dough is smooth and feels like pastry. Transfer to a square pan lined with waxed paper, pressing it out to a ¾ inch thickness. Bake at 350 to 375° for 30 minutes. Cut in small squares when half cooled; and remove from the pan. Cost: 86 cents.

English Food

It's not all roast beef and Yorkshire pudding for the people of the sceptered isle. English ingenuity has developed some mighty tasty and traditional delicacies over the past ten centuries or so. For example:

ENGLISH CHEESE PUDDING

1 quart milk
2 cups soft bread crumbs
1 teaspoon salt
¼ teaspoon pepper
2 tablespoons butter
2 cups finely chopped cheddar
¼ teaspoon baking soda
2 eggs

Preheat oven to 350°. Scald the milk. Add bread crumbs, salt, pepper, and butter, and stir until blended. Add the cheese, baking soda, and eggs, well beaten. Transfer to one large or six individual pudding dishes or ramekins rubbed with butter. Place in a pan of hot water and bake at 350° for 45 minutes, or until a knife when inserted comes out clean. Serves 6. Cost: $1.20.

ENGLISH SCRAPPLE

Good, hot, and cheap—that's a three-word description of scrapple, an old favorite but long forgotten breakfast food. Scrapple is merely a cereal made from some kind—almost any kind—of grain (cornmeal, oats, etc.) cooked and mixed with meat scraps, usually pork, and then cooled in a loaf pan, sliced and fried in butter, oil or bacon grease. It's wonderful on a chilly morning. It costs very little and makes a hearty way to begin the day.

Swedish Food

From Kristin Lavransdatter down, the Swedish people have made much of their sea-girded, chilly domain. Robust rye and tasty fish from icy waters are a mainstay of their healthful diet.

SWEET SWEDISH LOAF

1 compressed yeast cake
1 cup tepid water
1½ cups scalded milk
3 cups whole wheat flour
1 teaspoon salt
¾ cup melted butter
3 eggs
¼ cup honey
1½ tablespoons ground cardamom seeds
additional flour

Preheat oven to 350° or 375°. Dissolve the yeast in the water; add to the milk. Beat in the flour and salt. Cover and let rise until spongy. In another bowl beat together the butter or substitute, eggs, and honey, and add to the dough. Add half the cardamom seeds and the additional flour and knead. Transfer to long, narrow, buttered pans; cover and let rise until doubled in size. Bake at 350° to 375° for about 45 minutes. When almost done brush over with a cornstarch glaze, honey and the remaining cardamom seeds. To make the glaze, add two tablespoons cornstarch to one cup cold water; stir until it looks clear. Cost: $1.50.

A European Chicken-Saver

Fricassee is the traditional European dish designed for extracting the last and the best from an old, tired laying chicken (it works for old, tough turkeys too).

FRICASSEE

1 stewing chicken	3 tablespoons flour
3 cups water or stock	2 egg yolks
1 carrot	3 tablespoons cream
1 medium onion	fresh parsley, chopped
1 bay leaf	your choice of herbs
3 peppercorns	pinch of salt
¼ pound mushrooms	12 small onions, peeled
6 tablespoons butter	

Cut up the chicken; place pieces in a large cast iron pot and cover with 3 cups boiling water or veal or chicken stock. Add to the pot the medium onion, carrot, bay leaf, herbs, peppercorns and leek. Cover but allow steam to vent. Simmer until tender, usually 1 hour or more. Take out pieces of chicken, keep them hot. Strain stock and chill it. Meanwhile, simmer the 12 small onions and mushrooms in a sauce of 3 tablespoons butter and chicken stock. Now melt 3 tablespoons butter, stir in flour and add chicken stock. Cook gently for 10 minutes, remove from fire and correct seasoning. Combine egg yolks with cream. Place chicken on hot platter. Garnish with onions and mushrooms. Stir cream and egg mixture into hot stock. Return to stove until hot but not boiling. Pour sauce over chicken, garnish with parsley, and serve at once. Serves 6-8. Cost: $1.84.

Note: To stretch this dish, add some barley.

As the artificial food shortage closes in on all of us, we look to all the world's peoples for ideas and suggestions. We all share an ever-growing need for ingenuity and diligence in making much from little.

Healthful desserts from simple ingredients

What You'll Learn:
How you can enjoy delicious
no-sugar desserts at prices so low you
can serve them at every meal.

A good dessert must have several things going for it. First, it should look attractive. It's surprising how easy it is to pretty up good food. Always keep a mixture of walnuts, peanuts, cashews, chopped dried fruits, and sunflower seeds in an airtight container. Sprinkle a handful of the mixture over your finished desserts. They'll spark the appearance and taste of any sweet food. Raisins too are great for adding a little touch of sweetness to many desserts. So are fresh grapes and cherries.

Second, the dessert should be appropriate to the meal: a rich substantial dessert should top off a light repast and a light and airy one should end a robust feast.

Finally, desserts should add something wholesome to your diet. Since you are trying to eat better for less money, think of desserts as an important and integral part of your over-all penny-pinching meal plan. Here are some recipes to give your low-cost meals a special final touch.

BANANA SPICE BARS

These bars are light as cake, but solidly full of the crunch of sunflower seeds, peanuts, and soy grits. One bar provides 5 grams of usable protein, or 11 to 13 percent of the average daily requirement.

1½ cups mashed very ripe bananas	2 teaspoons cinnamon
	1 teaspoon allspice
2 eggs	½ teaspoon nutmeg
⅔ cup honey	½ teaspoon salt
¼ cup oil	¼ teaspoon cardamom
½ cup buttermilk or yogurt	1 tablespoon baking powder
¼ teaspoon almond extract	1 teaspoon baking soda
2 cups whole wheat flour	½ cup chopped peanuts
¼ cup soy grits	⅔ cup sunflower seeds

Preheat oven to 350°. Put the bananas, eggs, honey, oil, buttermilk, and almond extract into your blender; buzz until smooth. In a large mixing bowl stir together all the remaining ingredients; make a deep well and pour in the blender mixture. Combine the mixtures completely, but don't overmix. Pour the batter into two well-oiled 9″ × 9″ pans. Bake at 350° for 30 to 35 minutes, until the cake is well browned on top, dark around the edges, and pulls away from the sides of the pan. Cut into bars (approximately 18) while the cake is still warm; set the pans on racks to cool. Cost: $1.10.

(Thanks to Ellen Ewald and her *Recipes for a Small Planet* for this and the next four recipes.)

GINGERBREAD

A dark molasses gingerbread—delicious with yogurt and fruit. One piece provides 4 grams of usable protein, or about 9 to 10 percent of the average daily requirement.

1¾ cups whole wheat flour
½ cup soy flour, scant
½ teaspoon salt
1 teaspoon baking soda
2 teaspoons baking powder
1 tablespoon freshly grated ginger root
2 eggs, beaten
⅓ cup oil or melted butter
1 cup unsulfured molasses
¾ cup hot water

Preheat oven to 325°. Stir the dry ingredients together (include the fresh ginger root here, too). Stir the remaining liquid ingredients together. They won't blend very well, but we just want them to be together. Add the liquid to the dry mixture and blend with a few swift strokes. Immediately place the mixture in a well-oiled 9″ × 9″ baking pan. Bake at 325° for 30 to 35 minutes, until the cake is done. About 12 pieces. Cost: 71 cents.

FROZEN CREAM CHEESE AND YOGURT PIE

A luscious pie that's easy to assemble. Keep it frozen or it will turn to soup. Garnish with any fresh fruit that's in season. One portion provides about 5 grams of usable protein, 11 to 13 percent of the average daily requirement.

Make 1 9″ pie crust using 2 cups whole wheat flour, 2 tablespoons milk powder, ⅔ cup yogurt. Sift dry ingredients, cut in moist ingredients, mix and roll as in regular pastry recipe.

1 cup cream cheese, softened to room temperature—try to obtain cream cheese without additives such as vegetable gum

⅔ cup yogurt
¼ cup milk powder (⅓ cup instant)
½ cup honey
vanilla or almond flavoring, optional
fruit in season

Bake the pie crust at 375° for about 15 minutes. Cool it while you make the filling.

Beat the cream cheese and yogurt together with a wire whisk (or electric mixer, if you prefer) until the mixture is smooth. Whisk in the milk powder 2 tablespoons at a time; then whisk in the honey. (Add a few drops of flavoring if you wish. You might try lemon or orange, too.) Pour the filling into the cooled pie shell and put it into the freezer. If you are fond of frozen fruit, you may garnish the pie before freezing. Otherwise, when the pie is firm, garnish with fruit and then serve. Cost: $1.50.

BREAD PUDDING WITH LEMON SAUCE

Make this pudding with whole wheat bread or whole protein bread that has dried out a little. One portion provides about 8 grams of usable protein, or 18 to 22 percent of the average daily requirement.

2 cups dry whole wheat bread cubes
4 cups hot milk
½ to ⅔ cup honey
1 tablespoon butter
½ teaspoon salt
4 eggs, slightly beaten
1 teaspoon vanilla
½ cup raisins, optional

Preheat oven to 350°. Pour the hot milk over the bread cubes; while they soak, stir in the honey, butter, vanilla, and salt (and raisins). When the mixture has cooled slightly, beat in the eggs. Pour into an oiled 1½ quart baking dish. Place in a pan of hot water and bake at 350° for about 1 hour, until firm.

While pudding is baking prepare lemon sauce:

1 tablespoon cornstarch
dash salt
dash nutmeg
1 cup boiling water
¼ to ⅓ cup honey
1½ tablespoons lemon juice
2 tablespoons butter

Combine the cornstarch, salt, and nutmeg in a small saucepan; stir in the hot water gradually and cook over low heat until thick and clear. Blend in the honey, lemon juice, and butter. Pour over warm pudding and serve. Makes 8 portions. Cost: $1.10.

SPICED FRUIT RICE PUDDING

A rice pudding with a difference. One portion provides about 9 grams of usable protein, or 20 to 24 percent of the average daily requirement.

1½ cups raw brown rice
2½ to 3 cups milk
pinch salt
½ cup honey
½ teaspoon powdered ginger
2 cups of fruit (fresh or soaked dried apples, apricots, or oranges), coarsely chopped
1 egg beaten
½ teaspoon cinnamon
½ teaspoon nutmeg
2 tablespoons lemon juice
1 cup yogurt

Preheat oven to 350°. Cook the rice in a pressure cooker or regular saucepan, using milk instead of water. Use 2½ cups milk in the pressure cooker or 3 cups in saucepan. When cooked the rice should be tender but will look soupier than rice cooked with water. Stir in the honey, egg, cinnamon, nutmeg, and ginger. Oil a 1-quart casserole and spread ½ of the rice mixture over the bottom. Gently place ½ of the fruit chunks on top of the rice. Repeat the two layers and place in a 350° oven. Bake the pudding for 25 minutes. Remove from the oven and spread the 1 cup yogurt over the top. Chill several hours before serving. Cost: $1.20.

PEACH CRISP

6 cups fresh or canned peaches, drained
⅓ cup whole wheat flour
1 cup rolled oats
¼ cup honey
1 teaspoon cinnamon
⅓ cup melted butter or margarine

Preheat oven to 375°. Place peaches in baking dish. Combine dry ingredients, add melted butter, mixing until crumbly. Sprinkle on top of peaches. Bake at 375° for 30 minutes or until peaches are tender. Serve warm or cold with cream. To vary, substitute apples for peaches. Cost: 85 cents.

18

A checklist of money-saving hints

What You'll Learn:
Fifty-seven practical ways of combatting
high food prices.

Connie Donnellan is food editor of the *National Tattler*, an American weekly patterned after the old English Tattler of the 18th century. The latter was an outspoken, idol-smashing publication just like its modern counterpart. Recently, Connie published a group of food tips that were new and different...not the old stuff about keeping the mice out of the cookie jar. She has kindly agreed to allow a goodly number of them to appear here. Interspersed with Connie's tips are some from my book *How To Live In The New America*. Together they make a powerful inventory of fifty-seven methods and techniques to combat high food prices and make yourself more independent at the same time.

Meating the Crisis

When buying meat, it is false economy to pay high prices and find you have five ounces of bone per pound. It is wiser to pay more for a boneless, trimmed cut unless you plan to use the waste.

1. Save all meat bones and freeze for soup. Bones provide much more than a mere flavor base for soup. The natural gelatin derived from them is an important source of protein. Add a few teaspoons of vinegar to the water in which you simmer the bones to extract the maximum amount of high grade calcium.

2. When preparing meat, use the drippings to make gravy—even if you do not plan to serve it immediately. It can be frozen for later use to enhance rice or noodles for a meatless meal.

3. Save every scrap of leftover meat. Freeze to add to the soup kettle or combine with leftover potatoes and vegetables and freeze in discarded pans.

4. Render beef fat for deep frying and for use as shortening in vegetable and meat pies or biscuits.

5. Rendered pork fat may be used as a substitute for margarine or vegetable fat in baking.

6. Always save bacon drippings to sauté onions, potatoes and vegetables. It may be used in place of oil to dress spinach salad or to flavor potato salad. When preparing popcorn, bacon drippings may be substituted for oil to add a unique flavor. (If your doctor has placed you on a low cholesterol diet, using rendered meat fats is not advisable.)

7. Grow your own meat. Rabbits are easy to care for and will eat up all your vegetable scraps and convert them to protein. Prepare rabbit with chicken recipes. Tastes great!

8. For low budget scallops, buy shark from fishermen. Then cut the steaks into rounds with a cooky cutter. You've eaten these and never known it. Delicious!

9. Keep your mind open; horsemeat can be used in lieu of beef in any recipe and it's much cheaper. It's only prejudice that keeps people from using this high quality protein. Also, horsemeat is not doctored up with chemicals as is most beef and pork these days. Do your best to find range-fed cattle if you eat meat at all.

10. Somebody give you venison? Then grind it up with fat from other meat. This larding will eliminate the natural dryness of deermeat.

11. Do the same with bear, elk, moose and other wild game. Marinating in a vinegar-herb mixture does wonders.

12. Tough meat tip...just braise in wine as slowly as you can...a 250 degree oven would be perfect or use your fireless cooker.

Poultry Pointers

Except for rare occasions, poultry is generally a good buy. But you can get even more for your money by using it wisely.

13. When roasting a bird save the giblet, neck (avoid chickens that have hormone neck implants however) and other parts. Accumulate them in the freezer for use in soup or stock.

14. The carcass of a roast chicken or turkey makes a pot of wonderfully thick soup. When you have removed all of the meat, simmer the carcass in water with onion, celery, carrots and bayleaf for several hours. Pick remaining slivers of meat off the bones and add to soup. The marrow from the bones serves as a natural thickener. (Add some of your bulk rice or barley for even more value.)

15. Try the slow-roast method with older chickens. Low heat for long periods like a Spanish barbecue.

16. Most wild game birds such as pheasants and quail can be prepared in the same manner as chickens and turkeys. So be receptive to your hunter-friend's gifts.

Versatile Vegetables

17. Most of the vitamins and nutrients in vegetables are in or near the skin. And nearly all vegetables are edible from root to stem. So wash all vegetables before peeling, (if you must peel) place the parings in the freezer and wrap in cheesecloth to add to simmering soups. For stocks, no other vegetables are needed.

18. Don't throw away the dandelions from your lawn; you can eat both leaves and root, cooked or in salad.

19. Fennel grows in abundance all over the world. Collect it yourself and cook the stems like celery, add mushrooms, tomatoes and olive oil, Italian style.

20. Eggplant is usually a good buy and it's nutritious too. Tasty when stewed with onions. tomatoes and green peppers. Even better when prepared like a small steak; dipped in a fritter batter and sautéed. Adding Parmesan cheese makes them superb and even children, the fussy type, will eat them.

21. Wash and save vegetable trimmings such as carrot and celery tops, beet greens and onion tops. Add to eggs for a nutritious omelette or use to garnish soups and salads.

22. Add grated potato, cabbage or any vegetable to ground beef as an extender when making meat loaf or hamburger.

23. Fry potato peelings for a nutritious free snack. Serve hot or cold.

Your Dairy Dollars

With dairy foods skyrocketing over the past ten years, it's time to learn how to obtain the most from the least.

24. Powdered milk is your best buy. A dash of vanilla may be added to improve the taste or mix powdered milk with whole milk to stretch the quantity. Powdered milk tastes best when prepared a day in advance and refrigerated overnight before drinking.

25. Eggs, bought when they are less expensive, may be successfully frozen for use in baking or scrambling. Wrap the yolks and whites separately to freeze.

26. Whipping cream is expensive. Add a ripe, mashed banana to an egg white and beat until stiff for an economical substitute.

27. A low cost substitute for sour cream is yogurt. See the recipe given in another part of this book. Use yogurt on baked potatoes or any place where sour cream is often used.

28. With butter up and margarine not as healthy as it once was, stretch the real thing by whipping with evaporated milk or a rich mixture of powdered milk and water.

29. Eggs have the highest protein content per pound. Be sure they come from free-running, organically grown, happy chickens. Once you enjoy a real egg, you'll know the difference.

To The Last Crumb

30. Grind toast into dry breadcrumbs in your blender; soft breadcrumbs can be made from leftover bread or crusts. Store in airtight containers.

31. Make seasoned crumbs for many uses by adding dry minced onion, seasoned salt, pepper and/or herbs.

32. Use leftover, slightly stale bread as French toast. Dip in milk/egg batter and fry on hot griddle in a bit of butter or bacon drippings.

33. Many small bakeries will sell unbaked dough. As long as they use a healthy set of ingredients, buy some and bake your own bread, rolls, coffee cakes.

Do It Yourself and Save

Make-ahead mixes and prepared foods are convenient but they cost more. In many cases, you can make up your own combinations in bulk. And stored properly, they will keep indefinitely.

34. Seasoned rice is as easy as adding chicken or beef bouillon to the cooking water and stirring in herbs of your choice. You may wish to brown the rice in drippings first.

35. Seasoned salt is a combination of ¼ cup salt, 2 tablespoons paprika, 1½ teaspoons pepper, 1½ teaspoons onion powder.

36. Garlic salt may be made by crushing one or more cloves of garlic into the opening of a salt container.

37. Onion salt may be made by grinding dried, minced onion flakes to a powder in the electric blender and mixing to taste with table salt.

38. Save about 30 cents a pound by making your own noodles. Use a fork or slotted spoon to mix a cup of all-purpose flour with two eggs and 1 teaspoon salt. Roll thin, cut into strips and dry.

39. Make your own stove-top dressing using cubes of stale bread equivalent to ½ loaf. Add 1 packet of instant beef broth, 1 tablespoon poultry seasoning, 1 teaspoon chopped onion, ⅔ cup of hot water and 1 tablespoon butter.

40. Save up to 40 cents making your own tomato juice. To one small can of tomato paste (6 ounces), add celery seed, salt and enough water to make one quart; mix well.

41. Make your own cream soups by pureeing leftover vegetables and broth with evaporated milk in the electric blender. Worcestershire sauce or curry powder may be added to your taste.

42. Creamed salad dressing may be made by adding herbs, spices and/or cheese to yogurt.

43. Add vinegar and oil to nearly empty catsup or chili sauce bottles for french type salad dressing.

44. To make your own biscuit mix combine 8 cups whole wheat flour, 1⅓ cups non-fat dry milk, 5 tablespoons double-acting baking powder and one tablespoon salt (optional). Work in 1 cup shortening with fingertips until mixture resembles fine meal. Store in airtight container in cool, dry place.

45. Earn some extra money by canning wild blackberries with homemade labels. You'll sell all you make.

46. When strawberries are in season, find a roadside stand selling them by the flat.

47. Swiss chard is the most prolific plant you can grow in your backyard garden. Plant some soon and reap a continual harvest. Good cooked with salt, pepper and butter or cooked/chilled with any salad dressing.

48. Ever try set line fishing? Just bait some hooks on a single line, drop in the water from a bleach bottle float and go about your business. The fish will catch themselves and wait for your return.

49. For terrific onion rings, dip them in batter (beaten egg, milk and cornmeal), fry in vegetable oil. A mighty delicious and inexpensive main or side dish.

50. Dried cabbage rose leaves make a fine tea.

51. To hull sunflower, pumpkin or squash seeds, crush and stir in water. The lighter hulls will float and you can pour out the water to obtain the heavier seed kernels. Drain, dry and *voila*, you have a tasty, nut-like treat that is loaded with vitamins and minerals. This is an old Chumash Indian trick.

Saving Substitutions

52. Canned mackerel may be substituted for salmon, especially in casserole recipes.

53. Oatmeal makes a fine substitute for expensive nuts. A good example of the usage is in pecan pie.

54. Save money on baby food by pureeing meat, vegetables and fruits from your regular dinner with a little liquid for baby.

55. Save the pickle liquid for use in potato salad. Or when the pickles are gone, add fresh vegetables such as carrot sticks, onions, green peppers or cucumber to the jar and pickle your own treats.

Miscellaneous

56. Soak whole grain overnight. In the morning, grind it or place in a blender. Add raisins, nuts, dates or other good things. Eat hot or cold with or without milk and honey. Inexpensive and nutritious.

57. Is there a spaghetti factory near you? If so, buy their broken pieces for a fraction of the price of regular spaghetti. Sometimes they sell their "bends," the looped part, for very little. And they all taste just as good as the straights when cooked.

Render Your Own Lard

It's getting more difficult to obtain natural cooking fats. Most packaged varieties have chemical preservatives in them. So ask your butcher for pork fat scraps, take them home, cut them into small pieces, and slowly, very slowly, heat them until the fat runs out. (You can eat what's left of the pork if you wish; down South it's called cracklins.) Pour the rendered lard or hog fat into jars; seal and store in a cool place. Use this lard for everything from mixing your biscuit batter to frying your breakfast eggs. It's great in main dishes, particularly when frying is called for.

The World's Easiest (And Cheapest) Soup

Have you ever made more spaghetti sauce than you could use? Turn the surplus into a fine soup by diluting with a bit of water to bring it to the consistency you wish, add chopped celery, more onions, and as much broken spaghetti or macaroni as you like. Presto! Soup for lunch!

Beware The Forever Fruit

Did you hear about the maraschino cherry that was buried in the ground for a year and dug up good as new? That's just about what would happen to most supermarket foods if they were buried. So imagine how they must lie in your stomach daring a digestive juice to penetrate their preservatives!

While You're Thinking About Dinner

Just get home? Still debating what to have for dinner? Not much around to cook? Then onions to the rescue. While you're thinking and searching, peel and chop up one to four onions and begin sautéeing them in a heavy iron skillet using anything handy as the lubricant—butter, olive oil, or bacon fat. If you find some potatoes, toss them in. A bit of meat, fine; that can go in too. Some tomatoes? Great! In no time you'll have a delicious hot dish with flavorful, healthful onions as the base. Even if you don't find anything to add, sit down to a salad and a big bowl of freshly sautéed onions with salt and pepper and a hunk of crusty French bread and butter. Simple, yet noble fare.

Be Your Own Hamburger Helper

The main ingredient in most packaged hamburger additives is a cheap carbohydrate—potatoes or noodles. The sub-ingredient might be a small can of sauce and some spices. Good God, Gertrude, a can of sauce and some spices are well within your means, so make up your own hamburger additive. Buy noodles and potatoes in bulk, a case of tomato sauce and a selection of spices such as oregano, thyme, sage, parsley, rosemary, and basil. Now you're on your own at a fraction of the cost and no more work than doing it from the "handy" box.

Bill Kaysing

You Don't Have To Guess The Turkey's Age

When you're turkey shopping, here's how to determine age of the bird: young turkeys (for roasting) have black feet, three-year-old turkeys (set them free) have pink feet, and old turkeys (for soup) have grey feet. Incidentally, the ideal size turkey is 10 to 12 pounds.

Vegetarian Diet Anyone?

Some Chileans I've heard of carry 200 pounds of ore up a steep eighty-yard slope twelve times a day. These same people live on a diet of vegetables, figs, bread, and farrenai root (whatever that is). No meat. In Brazil, some coffee workers carry a bag of coffee weighing 180 pounds for a mile without resting. Breakfast is figs and bread, lunch boiled beans, dinner roasted wheat. You be the judge. Be advised.

Many nutrition experts tell us that meat has been oversold as a source of protein. It's expensive, acid-forming, and usually loaded with chemicals. According to a recent book, *The Secret Life of Plants*, meat sometimes has as many as 16 hormones, drugs and chemicals in it, none of which have a beneficial effect on the consumer. On the contrary, one in particular, DES (diethyl stilbestrol) is carcinogenic. Thus, with so many fine sources of vegetable protein available, it becomes highly conjectural whether meat should be eaten at all.

On a more positive plane, consider the facts presented in this same book regarding the radiations from various foods. As a basis, the radiations from humans is rated at 6,500 angstroms (an angstrom is a measure of wavelength). Foods are divided into four general classes, high radiation being preferable to low. Fruits and vegetables at the peak of maturity and freshness rate from 8,000 to 10,000 angstroms. They achieve the highest rating when consumed raw. Wheat has a radiance of 8,500 angstroms and rises to 9,000 when

cooked. Olive oil, butter (when fresh), and fresh seafood and fish also rate high: 8,000 angstroms and up.

In the second class of foods are such items as eggs, peanut oil, boiled vegetables and cooked fish. These rate from 6,500 down to 3,000 angstroms. Of meats, the only one to make the 6,500 and up category is freshly smoked ham. The others are "pointless to eat, an exercise in tough digestion which wears out rather than vitalizes the eater."

The third category includes all cooked meats, coffee, tea, jams, fermented cheeses and white bread. Because of their low radiation they do one little or no good. At the bottom; dead as far as radiation is concerned, are margarines, preserves, alchohol, refined white sugar and bleached white flour.

There are many fine books on vegetarianism versus omnivorism. These include:

Let's Eat Right To Keep Fit, Adelle Davis, Harcourt Brace Jovanovich.

Food Is Your Best Medicine, H. G. Bieler, MD, Random House.

Diet For A Small Planet, F. M. Lappé, Ballantine Books.

The Natural Food Cookbook, B. Hunter, Simon and Schuster.

The Complete Book Of Food And Nutrition, J. I. Rodale, Rodale Press.

The Secret Life Of Plants, Peter Thompkins & Christopher Bird, Harper & Row.

Study of these volumes will probably convince you that a strictly vegetable diet can be healthy. It is even more convincing to try a vegetarian way of life for several months. Then make your own decision. That's what I did and now enjoy a virtually meatless (and thus less expensive) way of life. Health and energy levels have never been higher!

Potluck Procedure

Everyone likes to take a break from the kitchen and go out to eat once in a while. Restaurants used to serve this purpose, but high costs and low income make alternatives more and more desirable these days. The old American custom of potluck dinners is returning, and a good thing, too. Here's how a potluck works. Everyone who participates in the dinner makes and brings a dish. It can be a salad, bread and butter, a casserole or other main dish, or dessert. Participants who don't have a way of cooking or bringing something are usually charged "a dime a dip," that is, ten cents for every portion they eat. The money charged goes to pay those who did bring dishes. Otherwise the potluck is free; your contribution is your payment. This is a good way to eat and enjoy other people's favorite dishes without the hassle of a dinner party. Cleanup is done communally too, and usually a good time is had by all. Potlucks are easy to organize. Just call up ten or twelve friends or newcomers to the community, set a time and place, and ask them to bring what they think others would enjoy eating. To avoid too many meat loaves or spaghettis, you can assign the items.

If Your Cupboard Looks Like Mother Hubbard's...

Down to your last dollar? We were one summer, so we bought nothing but potatoes and onions. We boiled up a batch of the spuds and used them with whatever else we could scrounge up. Often we caught a fish from San Francisco Bay (we were living on a boat) and fried them in some bacon drippings. When we acquired a little more money from odd jobs, we bought a twenty-five-pound sack of brown rice. We boiled rice for breakfast and added chopped fruit salvaged from the produce market. For lunch we had cold rice with bits of homesmoked fish and some soy sauce. Another big batch of rice was boiled up for dinner, and a mound of it was heaped high with more scavengings—this time celery and chard to make a passable imitation of a Chinese vegetable dish. Soy sauce helped out immeasurably; it lends a meaty taste to everything. Do

Bill Kaysing

you get the picture? Have some solid basic foods around with which to build the menu, meal, or snack. It's analogous to building a log cabin with the trees you find in a nearby forest. With the basic materials handy, it's not hard to provide the trimmings.

Recommended reading

It is strongly suggested that the reader who wishes to not only save money but enjoy better health take the time to study as many of these books as possible. Check the library or order through your local book store.

The Complete Book of Food and Nutrition. J. I. Rodale and staff. *Rodale Books*, Emmaus, Pennsylvania, 1961. (Now in its 10th printing). A monumental work by a most astute researcher who was probably zapped by the food industry for his efforts to alert the American people. Read it if you don't read another book in this bibliography.

Let's Have Healthy Children; Let's Get Well; Let's Eat It Right; Let's Cook It Right. *Signet, New American Library*. Bergenfield, New Jersey. These four books by the late Adelle Davis warrant a place front and center in your personal library.

Back To Eden. Jethro Kloss. The date of the original copyright is 1939, but material from this book has been extensively reprinted. *Longview Publishing House*, Coalmont Tennessee. Subtitled, *A Human Interest Story of Health and Restoration to Be Found in Herb, Root and Bark*, this quaint volume presents such homely advice as "Eat food as far as possible in its natural state." Advises against the use of aluminum pots and for the consumption of nuts instead of meat.

The Natural Foods Cookbook. B. T. Hunter. *Pyramid Books*, New York, 1961. Hard to believe that this has been around so long, but then it takes a while to sell a million copies. That should be recommendation enough.

Stalking the Wild Asparagus. Euell Gibbons. *David McKay*, New York, 1962. This and Gibbons' other volumes —**Stalking the Healthful Herbs**, **Stalking the Blue-Eyed Scallop**, and **Beachcombers Handbook**—are the top sellers about gathering wild things to eat. And as prices continue to rise on through the ceiling, Gibbons' books become ever more relevant; we can even forgive him for doing TV commercials.

An Herb and Spice Cookbook. C. Clairborne. *Harper and Row*, New York, 1964. A must for the person who wants lots of flavor in his non-meat diet.

The Gourmet Health Foods Cookbook. M. and O. Teichner. *Coronet*, New York, 1967. Divided into two sections, "Magic without Meat" and "Savor without Salt," this modest volume will add to your resources as a vegetarian and salt-free cook.

International Vegetarian Cookery. S. Richmond. *Arco Publishing*, New York, 1970. Covers the world effectively and cites some unusual ways of making vegetables taste like they should.

Foods, Facts and Fallacies. C. Fredericks, PhD. *Arco Publishing*, New York, 1969. The author has been a pioneer in the field of eating healthy foods; this book reflects recent research in nutrition and health.

The Soybean Cookbook. D. Jones, *Arco Publishing*, New York, 1971. Since soybeans are a worthy replacement for meat, the 350 recipes herein will extend your interest substantially in the good bean.

Get Well Naturally. Linda Clark. *Arco Publishing*, New York, 1972. Ms. Clark also wrote **Stay Young Longer** and cites the nutritional ways to better health and longer life in both volumes. Incidentally, Arco has a fine library of books on the subject; write for their catalog at Arco Publishing Company, 219 Park Ave. South, New York, New York 10003.

Deaf Smith County Cookbook. M. W. Ford. *Collier Books*, New York, 1973. This cookbook invites substitution of good food in your present recipes.

The Vegetarian Epicure. A. Thomas. *Vintage Books*, New York, 1972. More than 250 recipes that make vegetables taste good.

Vegetarian Gourmet Cookery. A. Hooker. *Scribners & Sons*, New York, 1973. Another good book on living without meat.

Diet For a Small Planet. F. M. Lappe. *Ballantine Books*, New York, 1971. This is the original book that revealed how you can put together vegetable proteins to make protein-rich meals without meats. An overall plan for eating less or no meat. A breakthrough that makes other cookbooks obsolete.

Recipes For a Small Planet. E. B. Ewald. *Ballantine Books*, New York, 1973. The companion volume to the blockbusting **Diet**. Read it by all means!

Middle Eastern Cookery. E. Zane. *Scribner & Sons*, New York, 1974. Turkish, Armenian, North African, and Persian recipes utilizing the traditional ingredients—kasha, chicken, fish, fruits, vegetables, rice.

The Sweet Life. M. Newman. *Houghton Mifflin*, New York, 1974. Without using a bit of sugar or refined flour or any milk, the author has created great desserts from fruit juices, whole grain flours, natural sweeteners and unrefined vegetables oils.

Mental Health Through Nutrition. T. R. Blaine. *Citadel Division of Lyle Stuart*, New York, 1974. The layman's guide to attaining and keeping mental health through nutrition. It's a study of how vitamin and mineral deficiencies are responsible for most of our physical and mental ills.

Cookbook For Good Nutrition. Carlton Fredericks. *Grosset & Dunlap*, New York, 1974. An old-timer in the struggle for better quality foods, Fredericks continues his mission to keep Americans from committing gastronomic suicide. A diversified book emphasizing that good nutrition can be fun.

A Basket of Homemade Breads. U. Norman. *Morrow*, New York, 1973. A highly pictorial how-to-do-it bread book.

The Vegetarian Menu Cookbook. E. Michaels. *Drake Publishers*, New York, 1973. Heavily illustrated, this book shows the great beauty of non-meat cooking.

Madame Wu's Art of Chinese Cooking. *Charles Publishing Co.*, Los Angeles, 1973. Aristocratic, well illustrated, and a handsome addition to a Chinese cookery library.

Chinese Cooking for Beginners. A. Schryver. *Dodd Mead*, New York, 1974. Combines interesting fresh vegetables and very small amounts of poultry and meat or fish; an excellent introduction to the world's oldest cuisine.

Encyclopedia of Chinese Food and Cooking. W. and I. Chang. *Crown Publishers*, New York, 1970. Useful for its inventory of Chinese ingredients, photographs and descriptions.

Making Your Own Cheese and Yogurt. M. Alth. *Funk & Wagnalls*, New York, 1973. And why not, if you have lots of milk around.

The Rodale Cookbook. N. Albright. *Rodale Press*, Emmaus, Pennsylvania, 1973. Photographically enhanced, this large volume reflects the careful thinking of the pioneer Rodale group.

The Organic Directory. *Rodale Press,* Emmaus, Pennsylvania 18049, 1974. An up-to-date listing of places to buy organic and natural food supplies. Both producers and purveyors are presented.

The N.Y. Times Natural Foods Cookbook. J. Hewitt. *Quadrangle Books*, New York, 1971. Over 700 recipes without artificial flavors, colors, or chemicals.

The Secret of the Seeds, Vegetables, Fruits and Nuts. B. Friedlander. *Grosset & Dunlap*, New York, 1974. How you can recognize, grow, buy, prepare, eat, and enjoy vegetables, fruits and nuts.

The N.Y. Times Bread and Soup Cookbook. Y. Y. Tarr. *Quadrangle Books*, New York, 1972. This book emphasizes a more natural way of living and a more basic way of cooking. Typical are Danish Cabbage Soup and English Cobblestone Bread.

Rock Island Line

Special Note: Want a catalog of over 2,500 books similar to these? Send your name and address to *ABC Health Books*, P.O. Box 5852, Denver, Colorado 80217.

Index